When Marriages Go Astray
Choices Made, Choices Challenged

When Marriages Go Astray
Choices Made, Choices Challenged

Lina Fruzzetti

Orient BlackSwan

RCS
Publishers

Published by
Orient BlackSwan Private Limited
1/24, Asaf Ali Road, New Delhi 110 002
E-mail: delhi@orientblackswan.com

And

RCS Publishers
40 Oxford Apartments, 11 I.P. Extension, Delhi 110 092
E-mail: rcspublishers@gmail.com

First published 2013

ISBN 978-81-923046-2-5

Typeset in
Goudy 11/13
by Eleven Arts, Delhi

Printed in India at
Glorious Printers, Delhi

Distributed by
Orient Blackswan Private Limited
Bangalore, Bhopal, Bhubaneshwar, Chennai, Ernakulam
Guwahati, Hyderabad, Jaipur, Kolkata, Lucknow
Mumbai, New Delhi, Noida, Patna

For my grandchildren,
Deven, Sophia, Suraya, Kieran, Aidan, and Charlotte

Contents

Contents

Acknowledgments

Building on previous research in Bishnupur and Kolkata on kinship and rituals, in this work I approach the construction of gender through an analysis of tradition gone astray. I address the lives of women through the choices they make, the discussions surrounding the unions into which they enter, and the emerging debates about violence against women. My central quest is to find out if, indeed, the making of the "new woman" emerges out of these inter-caste and inter-religious marriages I have followed. In studying mixed or "untraditional" marriages, I also attempt to contextualize what women mean by the concepts they use to justify their actions such as "rights," "freedom" or "our will to act in accordance to our desires." What do these words mean and what do they signify? Are they in fact redefining tradition?

I owe an immense gratitude to the women and men of Bishnupur who tirelessly continue to educate me and put up with my constant visits and questions that I still have not answered after forty years of research. In particular I would like to thank Subodh Ghar, my assistant, who persevered and saw me through various periods of my fieldwork in the town. This book is the result of 7 years of study, long interviews with couples about the meaning of their marriages and the problems they had experienced in the process and why they are often considered to be problematic in their society. Additionally, I received assistance from many courageous women who agreed to talk with me and gave extensive interviews. I am indebted to Aditi Sen for the long hours she put in into transcribing/ translating the interviews, and for the insights she offered during the different phases of the research. Portions of some interviews are incorporated into the text. My dear friend Salome Wawire was involved as a reader and she has helped to edit an earlier version of the manuscript. As an Africanist anthropologist, I value the questions she raised regarding Indian anthropology and issues of gender. These were helpful insights.

To Tricia Reville, I thank her for her efforts in helping me in my first attempts to arrange and sort out my research data. Sujaya Desai, an undergraduate at Brown, came to my rescue when she offered her assistance in sorting out my bibliographical work, prepared the glossary and made some editorial suggestions. Most of all I owe thanks to my friends at RCS Publishers, especially Aloke Roy Chowdhury, who has never failed to see my work through to its completion, and Joyati Sen's tireless and meticulous efforts in the editorial work she invests on any manuscript. How can one simply thank them?

My thanks also to my young friend Aamana Singh, who used her creative abilities and insights to come up with the cover design for the book. I am so thrilled to include her artistic qualities as part of my own work.

Funds for the different phases of the study were provided by various sources. To mention a few of these, I would like to acknowledge the support of the Brown University Vice President's Faculty Research Funds for the Arts, Humanities, and Social Sciences, and grants from Brown University President's Venture Fund for Faculty Innovation and from the Richard B. Solomon Faculty Research Award. The last three years I was fortunate to be awarded the Royce Family Professorship in Teaching Excellence. Some of the proceeds were applied to the completion of the manuscript. The research fund components were used to return to Bishnupur twice, using the trips to finalize the study, and to cover editorial work and other costs related to publishing. I owe the Royce family a huge debt for making this project possible.

Finally, and most important, a word of gratitude to my family, always understanding of the inordinate time I took away from matters relating to their needs to spend it in Bishnupur doing research on the project. It is worth it, I hope. To my husband Ákos, always the right critic of my work, but criticism I cherish. Nothing goes by without his words of encouragement and or disapproval of the written or conceptual aspect of the work. I thank you once again.

Lina Fruzzetti
Kolkata, 2013

Introduction: Reflections on Gender and Research in Bengal

"It was the nature of the woman's commitment to the conjugal order that bound the system together. Moral initiative therefore passes on to the woman, uniquely privileging her activism. If the household was the embryonic nation, then the woman was the true patriotic subject." Sarkar (2001: 43)

As a pre-doctoral student striving to understand the system of relationships and the construction of gender, I focused my study on gender and kinship in the town of Bishnupur. In that research, I was interested in understanding the ongoing debates about culture, tradition and the world of women. I focused on the so called "ideal image of a woman," which was driven by the pre-independence Indian nationalist movement for the preservation of the woman, nation and tradition, all of which notions were perceived to be represented by the same symbol. During this research, I did not expand my focus to include what was known as "the incarceration of women within the home," as referred to in an 1884 poem by an anonymous woman:

Free bird, how do you hope to be happy within the cage?
Imprisoned, you have forgotten your own speech.
And yet repeat the words of others mindlessly.
Narishiksha, part 11 (Calcutta, 1884: 76; quoted in Sarkar 2001: 46)

To begin with, my pre-doctoral research sought to examine the societal and traditional understanding of culture and gender constructs—the way women's behavior in society and in the home were scrutinized. This scrutiny was carried out in an environment in which there was little or no challenge to the prevailing perceptions about tradition and cultural expectations, most of which did not favor women. Thus, I made the study of life cycle rites, the meaning of kinship relations, the totality of the constructed person the main focus of my ethnographic research. *Gift of the Virgin, Concept of the Person* and *Kinship and Ritual in South Asia* are books that resulted from the first phase of my work, elucidating the meaning of being a woman within the cultural context of Bengali society.

Following the publication of these books, I deliberately took a 10-year break from conducting research in Bengal to start a new study in the Sudan. I was fortunate to return to India later, this time to work on a topic that focused on women's social and political movements in urban settings. It was during this study that I learned about the widespread problem of abandoned women and orphaned female children. I sought to understand the meaning behind the practice and concept. For example, I sought to answer questions such as: Who is or what *is such a person*, a woman who has no family? What does it mean to be a woman/girl/person who is perceived to be liminal in a structured society? How does an orphan, a woman with no social ties—kin, caste, community, religion—orient and define herself? Orphaned girls, often abandoned by their mothers' families, are housed in "homes."[1]

The above mentioned study, which was set in the mid to late eighties, would take me in new directions, a journey where concepts embedded in culture and steeped in Bengali tradition would give way to new approaches in the study of gender and society. The work with the orphan girls opened a new door for research that deciphered the meaning of the person considered liminal to society, structure and kinship. The presence of the orphan girls led me to questions about violence and abuse, and to the revelation of the *silent but powerful* strength of women in influencing their social situation and creating alternatives to traditional practices and perceptions.

In 1998, with the publication of *Women, Orphans, and Poverty: Social Movements and Ideologies of Work in India*, I completed my research work about the orphans. The revelation of unresolved and increasing gender-based violence in the community took me to the fundamental question of what role culture and kinship played in the construction of gender. I revisited my earlier research, this time focusing not on the disjuncture between the ideal and the reality of women's experience, but, instead, on how women's unorthodox and revolutionary actions attempt to redefine or challenge tradition and culture. Based on the data I collected, I found that there was a new conflict emerging: that between deep-rooted cultural perceptions and tradition, and emerging notions of alternative gender perceptions and relations. This period in Indian history, particularly in Bengal, was one of political and social turbulence, in which women were asserting themselves and letting their voices be heard in the continuing debates. An increase in the number of women who became victims of "dowry deaths"[2] was indeed a pointer to the importance of studying the experiences of women within such a society whose structure supports female subordination. However, it was also important to understand the meanings behind these practices, so I decided to reassess my earlier work in order to have a deeper understanding of the way this particular society operates.

For this phase of my research work, I draw from the research and scholarship of the nationalist, pre-independence period. Here, I seek to understand what it means to be a citizen/woman, and how women's bodies have altered the sites of national struggle to a battle for rights and entitlements, based on the shared, yet suppressed, discriminatory experience of women. "Notwithstanding significant changes in the cultural ideology of the ideal Hindu woman over the past decade or so, the image of woman as 'wife' continues to predominate within Hindu world view" (Fruzzetti and Östör 2007: 113). Given the increasingly deteriorating conditions in which women find themselves, along with increased incidences of gender-based violence, there does not seem to be enough attention focused on the fate and safety of women in this community. As such, there is a need to focus on research that continues to highlight these issues and challenge the status quo, which is based on outdated ideas that have persisted since before independence. Women continue to be viewed as symbols for the nation, and underlie what is understood to be family honor. For women, their concerns remain the children, the family, and the community, and increasingly, now, they are concerned about their self worth and happiness.

There is a growing literature of recent related studies on the subject of honor and women's complicit acts of disrespect or crossing the family bounds of "the right way to behave" (see Das 2000; Kandiyoti 1991 a and b; Ivekovic and Mostove 2006; Jayawardena and de Alwis 1996; Huq 2005). Failing to act in accordance to tradition is taken as a form of violation against the family, not dissimilar and instead synonymous to violence inflicted on women; the difference here is that a woman is inflicting the violence on her community. To act alongside one's cultural dictates, to unquestioningly obey because it is expected of them to do so, has confused women who felt they deserved better from the nation, instead they are trapped in the traditional world of imagery which supported the national ideal. For those who left their homes, the temporary return to structure makes a normally liminal anti-structure world permanent. In fact, given women's contribution to the nationalist cause, their own actions and lack of voice have strengthened the male role in the family, which is based on the male ideology that undercuts and subverts women.

Women and men acknowledged that the circumstances of women living in Bishnupur have been unquestionably altered. It was exactly eight years ago that I stumbled on an intriguing phenomenon—discussions linking the preponderance of inter-caste and inter-religious marriages taking place. Of every 1,000 marriages in the community, 800 were mixed unions. This fact alone, notwithstanding the reliability of the information, would surprise Dumont since he often mentioned in passing that marriage restrictions are the most resilient of caste hierarchy principles, and their easing would signal fundamental change (personal communication in numerous discussions). After the publication of my first book *The Gift of the Virgin* (1982), an ethnographical study about the ritual of marriage and kinship in Bengali society, it was time to reassess the meaning and the arrangements of marriages within the new discernment of caste and kinship.

In contrast to my earlier research conducted in the 70s, today, a younger generation of girls in their early twenties informs me differently; and they endeavor to educate me about their alternative choices in which they reposition themselves beyond the traditional marriage strictures faced and experienced by their parents. In the early 70s I interviewed the mothers of young marriageable women about the rites and traditions surrounding marriages. Today, I shift my attention to focus on the younger generation; the generations of children, whose mother's marriages were arranged and who were given away with a dowry, strongly elude attempts to replicate the earlier types of marriages underlying the double gift (wife and dowry) which define women. Thirty years ago, the question of marriage, was explicated by me as follows:

> Marriage is a sacred rite (*pabitra*) linking person to groups in terms of indigenous principles of and for action (where marriage, sacred ritual, person, and group are culturally constructed). Marriage also affects the meaning of the relationships among and between persons and groups, and the meaning of the categories to which these relationships refer (or, conversely, the locally understood relationships expressed by terms, symbols, and categories) (Fruzzetti 1982: 8).

In contrast to the earlier perception, the new unions are basically changing the meaning of the person, as well as the cultural constructions of marriage and gender understanding.

My new research continues and builds on earlier work within the same society where lineality, marriage and blood are central in one's consideration of alliance through marriage, in which womanhood is perceived to be accomplished and completed through the act of marriage. New unions question the structure of unions preceding them. They establish the unit of equivalence with one's own caste, though caste will not take center stage in their own negotiations for a partner. The strictures that are imposed by society in the marriage process provide the current generation with no choice but to make unconventional preferences that cross caste and religious lines.

Young unmarried girls have awakened to their dilemmas: culturally constructed and idealized as divinities in their everyday lives, yet, at times, they are exposed to violence and death threats, often through pressure demanding additional dowry or gifts from the married woman's family. In need of a solution, they make choices which are socially reviled. Short of remaining quiet to abuse or of encountering violence, these unmarried young women speak up, and confront the difficult issues as they occur. They do not continue to remain detached, as exemplified by earlier generations of women. They do not want to be victimized by the system, nor do they want to silently withstand abuse from violent spouses. Young girls are concerned about disengaging with the cultural disparity between the genders, and also to disaffiliate from beliefs which render them powerless. Without a doubt, women have challenged tradition: some have even gone further and renounced their faith, in which case, conversion would then allow them to marry a man outside of their faith. I will discuss inter-religious marriages and compare them to inter-caste marriages, both of which are seen as straying from cultural and societal perceptions of an acceptable marriage. In all of these mixed marriages the question of dowry payment is absent; it is neither given importance nor discussed by the consenting partners. But the alarming increase of these mixed unions begs the question as to what will be the fate of religion and caste within Bengali society? What will be the new definitional terms of and for identification within this society?

Townspeople acknowledge that women's fate has improved. All allude to the availability of education, which has provided women with additional support in their endeavors. This point will be part of the focus of the discussion in the following pages. The majority of employed women are either in government service or in the teaching profession. In past marriage negotiations, preference was given to an educated girl, along with her being fair-skinned, having long hair, goddess like beauty, poise and femininity. However, little importance was given for a career-minded woman. Today, for a woman to be gainfully employed increases her chances for marriage, irrespective of her caste, religion or looks. In addition, she herself makes the choice of a partner.

Dowry has kept increasing over the years, and continues to bankrupt families, especially those with more than two daughters. For the present generation, education is a way out; it provides them with the capacity to earn money that would enable them to pay dowry and follow tradition. At the same time, education provides brides with an alternative, although it is often frowned upon by society. Unmarried girls use their schooling to get information that would allow them to widen their horizon, and consider alternative options available to them. Thirty years ago, a woman working in a bank would worry about her chances for marriage. Today, the job itself allows her to negotiate a good marriage. In addition, unlike her parents' generation, a working woman today would be least concerned about marriageability. Inability to marry properly according to tradition is no longer a primary concern for women whose intention is to not adhere to an ostensibly conservative code of conduct that is dictated by their family. Even widows are marriageable today, especially those whose fathers can offer a hefty dowry or if the widow is employed. In short, I found that tradition and the strict codes of conduct for unmarried and married women have changed.

I embarked on the study of change by first addressing what had transpired in the last 35 years that has so fundamentally influenced the institution of marriage in directions contrary to the local traditions. One of the issues that surfaced dealt with the availability of education for females, not precedence for men. Women are not expected to be nor confined to the domain of the home. Today, young girls seek an education before the issue of marriage is raised. Unlike in the past, the girl's mobility outside the house is not restricted after she has achieved puberty, a life cycle rite after which it was deemed to be a dangerous state for the young unmarried girl. Whereas in the past, girls were not allowed to mingle or be in the vicinity of men outside their house, today one sees them in the company of male friends at all times. It is not surprising to find girls conversing with and at ease in the company of men, a practice that today does not lend itself to negative rumors as was the case in prior times. What was said to cause the demise of or bring dishonor to one's family and their daughter seems to be outdated today. Girls move about the town freely and nobody is shocked or eager to circulate gossip about the girls. In short, the fear of repercussions attached to such behavior in the past seems to have disappeared today. Discussing the idea of women's freedom was not a thing that girls were allowed to do, nor did they enjoy doing so. Today, they seem to share the same level of openness experienced by lower class women and those from the lower castes, working and negotiating a life in the public domain, office, schools or in the market.

In the past 35 years women have altered the way they live, operating under a different code of conduct, in contrast to the upper castes and classes which forbade their daughters the freedom to move out of the house. Keeping girls in ignorance of the outside world was purposeful, to be able to manage their life in accordance with family tradition, practices held sacred and meaningful to the women. Today, young girls are not as involved with upholding either the *brata*[3] tradition or the *meyder acar*,[4] which their mothers observed. These changes pertain to the protagonist, the young girl, who is conscious of her own interests, managing and orchestrating her life on her own terms, moving beyond the family guidelines for appropriate codes of conducts. They are not dependent on their elders, and it is almost impossible for them to be misled. Many of them attend college and some go beyond the Bachelor's degree level. School going girls have neither the time nor the inclination to perform the specifically female-related rituals their mothers did in the past, oblivious of the parental expectations in following the same tradition. Education absorbs all of their time; knowing well that only through education they can better their condition, they have made it their number one priority. As such, they remain focused on receiving an education, and to using the degree to acquire a position in the job market. One finds young women in many positions in varying professions today, many of which were not taken up by women thirty five years ago. Government service, nursing schools and college teachers, including a handful of women in the market economy (previously a male dominated world) offer women alternatives to being at home. Open competition for these jobs has allowed women to successfully compete for them. Their ambition is high, and their fight or resolve to succeed has clearly shown their intent to all around them.

In the past, marriage was the primary concern of a young unmarried woman. Coming across the challenges women experienced in the past and which, to some extent, still continue today, they were forced to rethink their priorities. The increase in inter-caste marriages not only raises concerns in a traditionally restrictive society and but also raises the need to investigate what happened to produce these changes? Establishing and finding gainful employment, for many young girls today, replaces the anxiety of having to learn what the proper code of conduct for a woman should be. A permanently employed woman is an attractive prospect for marriage, even for an unemployed man. I was curious to find out if this so called "rebellion" (as a woman referred to it) would translate to an idea of freedom on the part of these young girls. Do they experience liberation from tradition?

The idea that young or older unmarried women can have the option to decide their fate positions this change as a major advancement and achievement that one can barely begin to surmise. The search for the ideal groom is replaced by having a job. Yet, marriage remains the ultimate realization in this entire exploration. Women who are gainfully employed might allow their parents to arrange their marriage or take the step to do their own search, while an impoverished unmarried girl from an upper caste family might consider marrying below her caste if the groom is employed. Both of these marriages could have resulted from being in love with a person outside one's religion or caste, or it could be a marriage of convenience.[5] For some of the lower caste employed males, the idea of a wife from an upper caste family, even if it is without the payment of dowry, is an attractive proposition. After five years of studying this topic, my research highlights the increasing number of inter-caste marriages, along with a few inter-religious marriages, despite the fact that most families deny that such practices take place within their own families. The reasons for denial and refusing to accept the idea of inter-religious marriages in their family are based on the premise that there is a stark ideological difference between Islam and Hinduism, which are the two main religions in play in this area. Most of the women who enter into a marriage across religious lines are Hindu, and a handful of husbands allow their wives to observe their respective religions, a piece of information that I found men very willing to share with outsiders like me, in order to give the impression that they were open-minded.

The changes and the challenges: tradition, its strictures, and the dowry question

This current research touches on the underlying topic of dowry and, subliminally, on the fear of gender-based violence, especially when one's marriage is arranged with a stranger. In addition, having to move out to an unknown space to begin one's married life with new relations is a daunting challenge for a young woman. The media has clearly shown evidence of the occurrences of violence some young brides have been subjected to after their marriage. The assurance of a safe journey to one's in-laws' home that their mother's experienced is not guaranteed for women today. Moving out of one's parental place or village is negotiated and contested by contemporary young girls.

My study demonstrates that young girls, who now surf the internet, read the papers, tune in to watch dramas on TV and so on, are more aware and conscious of their limitations after marriage. A few young women openly articulate an existing disconnect in societal image and constructs of the good woman when they juxtapose their own vulnerability regarding violence and abuse which they often endure or have heard of from other women's experiences. Working with both Muslim and Hindu women who find themselves on the margins, symbolically and physically, who have challenged and resisted carrying the national banners for nation and family, has revealed to me the newer constructed, defiant, and difficult approaches that are employed by women to decode conflicting issues and to resolve them. They abhor the idea of rebound and returning to their mothers' culture, or way of doing things. The issue of dowry, an institution which is abolished and yet exerts extensive influence on which women can expect to marry, is stifling chances for marriage for many unmarried women. Furthermore, unmarried women have begun to ignore and publicly reject their cultural traditions so ardently observed by their parents' generation and caste members.[6]

Hindu women in the town ostensibly began to question their place in the nation and what constituted the rights of women through their actions, often seen as hostile to societal norms. When Muslim men choose to marry non-Muslim women, the Jamiat-il-Islam (community of Muslims) chastises the individual and repeatedly requests that the couple move out of their neighborhood. Of course, in the cases of conversion, where the Hindu bride converts to Islam, the couple is accepted within the fold of the Muslim community. Likewise, in the case of Hindu women who marry against their parental wishes, they too face the consequences of being ostracized, less so for inter-caste marriages and fiercely harsh if they cross religious lines. What rights do women have and who controls them? What are the boundaries of tradition and what does it mean to be a rightful citizen in a democratic nation? I will address these and other related questions in this book.

Attempting to decipher the post nationalist question of women's rights or responsibility, I embark on an effort to engage with the meaning and discourse of inclusive citizenship regarding women. The deteriorating and often unbearable conditions which women are forced to endure, coupled with an increase in gender-based violence, it is clear that women's experiences, fate and safety have not been adequately addressed. My current study also reveals how many women were unaware of their rights, and in the case of younger women, fear of recrimination held them back from seeking the law to protect themselves. In a sense, one could attest to "... the nature of the woman's commitment to the conjugal order that bound the system together. Moral initiative therefore passes on to the woman, uniquely privileging her activism. If the household was the embryonic nation, then the woman was the true patriotic subject" (Sarkar 2001: 43).

The study on mixed marriages and the fate of women who dared to undertake non-traditional marriages resonates with Shireen

P. Huq's work in Bangladesh, research which examines the pattern of everyday life and the centrality of violence against women, inside the domestic sphere and beyond those boundaries, inclusive of ". . . wife beating, dowry deaths, assaults, rapes and, more recently, *fatwa*-related violence and acid attacks, [which] are common" (Huq 2005: 169). In the less populated Muslim areas in rural Bengal, *fatwa*-related violence is not as yet a reality or an option. Women who are deemed to be contemptible and or shameful to their Muslim society will have force used against them, and communal consensus to be socially and publicly ostracized and banished from their community. These decisions borrow largely from results of national cases of women who have been shamed under similar circumstances. Looking at the recent honor killings in parts of north India, the case can be made for Hindu women who experience similar violent outbursts when their behavior challenges male privileged ideals for its women. The works of Patricia Jeffrey and Amrita Basu (1998); Patricia and Roger Jeffrey (1996); Ketu Katrak (2006); Diane Miller (1999); Henrietta Moore (1999) address the complexities of culture and the imposition of tradition in negotiating women's actions within the narrow boundaries of acceptability.

From the villages to the cities, we begin to hear women's voices questioning their representation in the national debates of citizenship as women, whether they are Hindus or Muslims. If, in fact, the female body is ". . . still pure and unmarked, loyal to the rule of the *shastras*" (Sarkar 2001: 43) what does the future hold for these women? Fundamentally, we find that women who consider themselves members of a society begin to question their role within the family and their rights over their bodies and choices. A few significant works addressing issues of women's rights juxtaposed against cultural impositions include Nira Yuval-Davis and Pnina Werbner (2005); Patricia Ulbrich and Joan Huber (1981); Lorraine Code (1991); Paromita Chakravarti and Kavita Panjabi (2011); and especially the relevant and crucial studies of gender by Maitrayee Chaudhuri (2003, 2004 and 2011). Central to their thinking is the question of whether women should remain immersed and relegated to a silenced space in the twenty first century. A few prominent studies make the connections between the subject woman and rights afforded to her by the state. Debates about formal citizenship enabled feminists to expose the contradiction between the state's constitutional declarations of equal citizenship and its treatment of women as the possessions of their husband or communities. In this I draw from the works of Rajeswari Sunder Rajan (2004); Rajlakshmi Sriram and Arun Bakshi (1988); Suruchi Thapar-Bjorkert (2006). Additionally, works by Diane Miller (2004) on violence within marriage; Satadru Sen and James H. Mills (2004) or Anne McClintok et al. (1997) attest to the unchanging condition women continue to encounter within a culture that eulogizes while violating the trust. Recently I came across an educated woman, Jaya, who actually equated herself to a caged bird. Jaya lamented that her life was reminiscent of being incarcerated within the home, referring to the poem quoted at the beginning of this chapter.

Containing femininity within the constraints of the private denotes a less empowering role for women in contrast to what Partha Chatterjee refers to in his *Nation and its Fragments* as the material world men occupy. Honor of the family was tantamount to the honor of the nation. Combining the two symbols left little room to negotiate, resolve the distinction, or lessen the responsibilities for women. When a woman violates her roles, crosses the boundaries of the home and the world, breaks the family tradition and challenges the concept of honor, she violates the traditional code of conduct. Her actions are synonymous to the violence inflicted on women; in this case she has inflicted them on her community. Today, society addresses the question of violence against women because women, through their actions, have influenced its importance in contemporary society. Similarly, there is a growing new scholarship that views women not as victims of violence, but as people who inflict violence on their own community.

Sreeparna Bhattacharya, in her recent work on the slum of Mumbai, observes that "Feminine virtues of perseverance, suffering, patience and non-violence were invoked in the male-dominated nationalist struggles by leaders such as Mahatma Gandhi. India was likened to a mother, to a goddess who was both strong as well as in need of protection, especially protection of her modesty which was being outraged by the British colonists" (2007: 115). This strong nationalist message and the accompanying discourse left women confused, trapped in the traditional world imagery in which the idea of nationalism was viewed as ideal. At the same time, their own lack of voice or tacit silence strengthened the male ideology that simultaneously undercuts and subverts women. Bhattacharya's urban slum work addresses the pain that women endure silently when faced with gender-based violence. She adds, "Social ostracism here is subjectively experienced and embodied through the boycott of members of one's community, with or without the consensus of the larger community" (ibid: 235).

Women successfully centered the debate of women's rights within the national space; positioning their concerns to parallel those of the nation. If the nationalists used the "woman" as the symbol in the fight for independence, establishment of the nation and the freedom of its citizens, the nation now owes women the attention they deserve. Where do they stand as citizens? Naila Kabeer's edited volume (2005) seeks to unravel the underlying meaning of citizenship, what it signifies to the ordinary people, what inclusive rights mean to those who see themselves as outside the circle of true citizenship, particularly when addressing women's rights. Shireen P. Huq's excellent work *Bodies as Sites of Struggle: Naripokkho and the Movement for Women's Rights in Bangladesh* touches on the shared sentiments and yet silenced discrimination women experience daily. Women engaged with her work reiterate their plight, and she adds "We had no idea of the intensity of the sense of injustice that lay beneath the surface, ready to explode. Many women had literally never spoken about themselves before" (Huq 2005: 166). A woman run movement, Naripokkho revealed that generally women were unaware of their rights, and opening women's eyes to the injustices has explicitly shown ". . . how much of the discrimination, ill treatment and violence women suffer is connected to the ways their bodies, their sexuality, their reproductive roles and their health are perceived, valued and constructed by their families, their colleagues and by society at large" (ibid: 167). Some of the women in my previous work were seen as ". . . pawns in a game that did not recognize the art of balancing gender inequalities, thus casting and effectively keeping women in a peripheral status. The absence of a recognized position attesting to women's contribution to society and the nation left voiceless women in an invisible space" (Fruzzetti and Tenhunen 2005: 11).

We do find women scholars today making the connections between state and gender, particularly debating the question of what citizenship entails for women. A study which stands out for me is Ritu Menon's essay titled "Do women have a country?" In many ways, Menon's work resonates with part of my current research. In addressing Hindu–Muslim marriages in rural Bengal, often the Hindu woman is perceived as a victim, an abducted woman. Menon makes an interesting argument tying the rights of Hindu widows and abducted women during Partition to the state, not their families: "As with sexuality, the debates around citizenship, too, were explicate in the case of abducted women; implicit—or shall we say, assumed—in the case of widows" (Menon 2006: 53). Her argument reveals the liminal position of the abducted women during the Partition period. To whom does she belong and whose responsibility is she? More than 66 years later, we revisit and reopen the wounds of Partition with regard to Muslim men who marry Hindu women (both of them willingly entering into the marriage). Interestingly, in the historical perspective, the case of the abducted Indian woman implies that she had the right as a citizen to act independently (and autonomously—of *her* community, state and family). Menon's conclusion is that the women were disillusioned yet convinced of the need to think about ". . . preserving community and national honor, by subordinating their rights as individuals and the will of the state" (ibid: 54). Using the metaphor of an inflexible boundary, women were again reduced to nationalist symbols of nation and religion, both in need of protection and preservation of the inner core of tradition. Returning to the primordial center of identification, the boundaries now are narrowed.

In another scholarly account, "Globalization and the Gendered Politics of Citizenship," Jan J. Petteman states that being a citizen (or not) seems to be a contested male identity that is constructed through the state. She comments, "Citizenship constructs a public status and identity—long presumed to be male—that rests in ambiguous ways on the private support world of family, home and women" (2005: 207). Srimati Basu (1999), Chandra Talapade Mohanty (2003), Sangeeta Ray (2000), Satadru Sen and James H. Mills (2004) are a few authors whose works corroborate my analysis; authors who question the rights of women given their contribution to nation and society. Similarly, Petteman's words resonate with earlier studies with reference to the nationalists' work and the women's movement during that period (Fruzzetti and Perez 2002).

Notes

1. Note the use of the English word "homes" in contrast to the Bengali concept of "*bari*" and "*ghar*," accompanied by an extensive kinship code of conduct and relationships.
2. Dowry deaths relate to deaths of young brides caused by poisoning or otherwise killing the bride. Often, a young bride might take her own life, to avoid the extreme pressures she has to endure from her in-laws requesting additional monies from her parents.
3. *Bratas* are specifically women's rituals worshipping diverse numbers of gods and goddesses.
4. "Women's rituals," these rituals are the practice of the rites which apply only to married women with a living husband.
5. Marriage of convenience implies that a man and a woman would decide to marry for a particular reason other than love.
6. By tradition I mean all of a family's or caste's value system, beliefs and cultural specific acts that distinguishes one family from another, one caste from others.

Caste, Marriage, and Challenges to Traditional Rites

"I abhor the caste system. I have not married any caste; I have married an honest, moral, sympathetic affectionate man." (Chitra Interview 2005)

The choice to marry: emergence of inter-caste unions

In the 66 years since India's independence, we have observed changes to the caste system in which questions of commensality and occupation have undergone drastic changes. Unlike before, one's caste-specific identification does not necessarily have connections to the original caste-based occupation. For example, it is now common to encounter a person who is from a caste of "sweepers" working in an office as a secretary, or a brahman working as a shopkeeper. Nonetheless, there was an understanding of an assumed constant, which supported the idea that the caste system was an enduring entity. Marriage, supposedly the stronghold of the three aspects of caste and a sacred rite of the Hindu social structure, has been undergoing change as well. In this chapter I will address the changes to the caste system, which, although abolished, still thrives in Hindu rural and urban societies. What causes the changes and how do we understand these alterations? Interestingly, the question of women's unequal status and the payment of dowry are attributed with initiating the transformations. The alarming increase of inter-caste and inter-religious marriages raises questions about the contradictions within the traditional Hindu social structure. This chapter focuses on the debate on inter-caste unions.

Without a doubt, the sacredness of a Hindu marriage as one knew it in the town of Bishnupur has been revolutionized as a rite of passage. While seeking to understand the depth of the structural changes, principally those that might have influenced women's lives, I was confronted by men and women of the town with a variety of ideas, discussions, and views concerning the subject of marriage. The narratives provided indicate that women's lives have experienced major changes, and also shed some light on the specific changes that have taken place. I sought to find out if the increase of mixed unions was linked to expanded freedoms and choices that are now available to women. Equally important was to find out the underlying causes or the principal reasons for the kinds of marriage that are currently predominant in the town. What does it mean to be confronted by increasing numbers of inter-caste unions for a town that prided itself on religious orthodoxy and the preservation of family traditions?

Alternatives for women:
Life with a choice for a partner

It was difficult to get an answer to the question whether there are allowable and acceptable alternatives for women other than marriage. The overwhelming majority of women I have interviewed underscore the importance of marriage for unmarried women. Mothers share a common fear that, in the absence of living parents, their unmarried daughters would have nobody to support them. Mothers believe that it is better for a woman to endure unhappiness, pain, and troubles in her marriage, as long as she is considered to be within the territory of her in-laws as a married woman. Sonali, one of my respondents, said: "If my daughter completes her education and takes up a job and is self-reliant, I have no objection. However, if unemployed and does not want to get married, who will be responsible for her after we die? In our absence, no one, neither uncle nor aunt, will look after her. Now we live in a joint family, but that might break up or disintegrate. Everyone will be on his own, setting up individual nuclear units. No one will look after the other. Being the only daughter, she does not have an older or younger brother. In a clash of self-interest, even your own become enemies. No one will take care or help" (Sonali Interview 2005).

Parents worry about the protection of their unmarried daughters. Families are aware of the stigma attached to the presence of unmarried girls in their father's house. Sonali explained: "People will indulge in gossip, but if she works and earns an income, people won't comment because she is a 'service holder,' independent, with her own income. There are single women who are service holders, but their relatives will look after them because they have bank balances and property. Working daughters are independent and will be able to manage their life" (ibid). Many mothers across caste and class expressed similar concerns.

The acceptance or rejection of an inter-caste marriage depends not only on the couple's caste, but also their social class. It seems that upper class families are lenient when their daughter marries a lower caste man whose family is wealthy, or is in the upper class. On the other hand, a son who marries a girl from a poor background usually runs into problems, especially if the son expects that his family accept her into their ancestral house. Families always attempt to match the class of the incoming bride. Class seems to be a major factor in determining the acceptability of the bride into the groom's family and ancestral home.

The theme that emerges from many interviews is the importance of class and caste differences, and the attached guidelines regarding socially constructed spaces. What constitutes a space and what makes it sacred? What are the taboos and impurities that would affect the culturally delineated spaces that would forbid the inclusion of a bride from another caste or social class? Introducing a bride, a woman from a different caste, whether from a lower or higher caste, poses challenges for the receiving family.

Inter-caste and inter-religious marriages do create tensions and crises, some of which are never resolved. By marrying against the family's recommendations, and by not marrying within the family's caste, Rupa's husband's was not allowed to enter the ancestral home. Since he crossed the boundaries of marriage acceptability with his inter-caste marriage, he lost his rights to his family. In turn, his inter-caste marriage, judged as a denouncement of the family's honor, barred him from any life cycle rites observed in his father's house.

Rupa's fault was in marrying a man from the Tambuli caste (betel leaf growers caste), a higher caste than hers. Her in-laws would not accept the couple into their ancestral house, so the newly married couple had to build their own house on the outskirts of the town, next to the burning *ghats* (the cremation grounds). Rupa was born into the lower Dhopa caste (washerman caste), also known as a scheduled caste. Her father practices his caste trade and has a laundry business where he washes and irons other people's clothes. Her husband, a Tambuli businessman in the wholesale and retail fruit trade, belongs to an affluent, large and well-established business family of the town. Clearly, there is a substantial economic and social gap between the two families.

When the couple sought permission from their respective families to get married, the families pleaded for them not to consummate the marriage—his family remained determined to ensure that the marriage did not occur, but the bride's family reluctantly accepted the union, even though they did not approve of her choice of partner. Her inter-caste marriage did not hinder or complicate her brothers' or sisters' marriages (something which is always feared by other families). She said: "None of my siblings have ever blamed me in any way. I have married a Hindu man, who is of a higher caste, and since I haven't married into a lower caste, my family has never blamed me, but had I married a Muslim they would have. I wouldn't have been allowed to enter the house and they would never have accepted it from their heart" (Rupa Interview 2005).

Rupa said about her husband's family, "Both of us pleaded for their permission and tried to request them not to forbid us (from getting married). My husband declared that he 'will not marry anybody else'" (ibid). Like many of the "mixed" marriages,

Rupa's marriage took place in the Bishnupur Registrar's office without the consent of the couple's parents. They had neither a celebration, nor a ceremony in the temple. Nobody was invited to their wedding, even though her own family accepted the union. They had left town to visit a friend's house for one month. Upon their return, and because of Rupa's inter-caste marriage, they were confronted by a tense atmosphere in Chakbazar (the local market), a site where Rupa's husband's family has a strong presence. Two months into the couple's marriage, the in-laws tried to break it up. Rupa said, "My in-laws are extremely rich, they have wealth and power, a family that has a lot of businesses in the market. On the other hand, my parents are poor; my father has a laundry business in the market, washing people's clothes for his livelihood. My father-in-law succeeded in causing a lot of trouble for my family and nobody protested against this injustice. All the people in the market enjoyed the harassment as silent spectators and my father could not defend himself" (ibid).

Young unmarried girls seek to secure their own future by attaining the status of "married women," given the fear of stigmatization by a society that does not approve of unmarried women. As such, many girls depend on their parents to arrange their marriage. Mrs. Sonali, one of the respondents, who was herself married at the age of nine years, expresses her concern about the future of her 14-year-old daughter. Mrs. Sonali lost her childhood due to her early marriage, yet she strongly supports and debates on the merits of marriage in a Hindu society. As she entered her in-laws' house at the tender age of 9 years, the separation from her own family was painful. She completed all the rituals of marriage before returning to her father's house until she became of age. She says, "My father chose an auspicious date and also fixed a date on which he took me to my in-laws; they (my family) had to spend a lot of money on gifts for my in-laws. This ceremony is called *dwiragaman* (returning again), because my parents were sending the bride to her home on an auspicious day for the first time. Now, girls get married and go to their in-laws house (*sosurbari*), and return for a visit to their parents place on *astamangala* (on the eighth day). I was treated well in my marital home and my mother-in-law used to love me like her daughter" (Sonali Interview 2005). I discovered that a large number of the older women interviewed in my study had their marriages arranged. The older women are faced with anxiety and fear when it is their turn to orchestrate marriages for their daughters. This is because they are cognizant of the importance of giving away their daughters in marriage, but also aware of the lack of guarantee that their daughters would be content and well in such unions.

Without a doubt, girls are challenging the tradition of arranged marriages; some girls choose to commit suicide than be given away in marriage against their will. Parents are constantly debating how best to address this predicament: should they force an arranged marriage or accept their unmarried daughters' alternative decisions? Many parents are cognizant of the increasing violence and abusive acts leveled against women. The images they view on TV have reiterated and confirmed some of their fears. Families are sensitized to the occurrences of torture and violence inflicted on brides, but those who have not experienced such heinous acts tend to ignore its seriousness. Of course, there are exceptions to the injurious experiences that one hears about from some of these marriages. A bride is lucky if she enters a peaceful house, to find a gentle mother-in-law, instead of an aggressive, harsh or abusive "mother".

Marriage, dowry and the search for a partner

Women are hindered from acting freely or voicing their opinions within a tradition that supports practices that devalue women. These practices affect women across class and caste, the effects of which highlight the inability of their society to face the challenges and make resolutions that would improve the status of women. An elderly woman explained why women are experiencing an increase of gender-based violence, and also an increase in reported rape cases. Although dowry is outlawed it persists under different guises, making it impossible for women to be married without the payment of dowry. Wealthy families demand dowry despite the fact that they are in no need of such resources. Many women ask why these rich families still need money attained from dowry. The women point out that there is an increase in greed, especially with the manifold increase in the amount demanded for dowry. This trend begs the question as to whether women are sold as commodities, as in a "bride market" where brides are put up for auction. Furthermore, there is no guarantee that more dowry translates into a peaceful and lasting marriage. An old brahman widow noted that her father paid a hefty dowry to her extremely wealthy in-laws. She entered a new house as a bride, having paid her "entrance fees" (implying the dowry). Yet, she encountered abuse and violence at the hands of her in-laws. She was lucky to escape further torture or death, though similar incidents have not happened to other brides joining the family after her. However, she has heard of cases where young brides are killed by their in-laws as a result of tensions arising from demands for more dowry or unpaid dowry dues. In one case, a young bride was burned by her in-laws; subsequently they were arrested, and at the time of this study, they were still awaiting trial. In another incident, the bride was poisoned because her father could not pay the balance accrued from dowry. At the time of the study, the perpetrators were held in jail, awaiting trial.

Uncertainty about the identity of the husband/life partner as well as the apprehension about fitting in with the in-laws is a situation that is experienced by many young unmarried women. A majority of the unmarried girls I interviewed depended on their own judgment to make the right selection of a partner. Marrying within one's own caste was not a guarantee that one would be happy. Women continue to endure multiple forms of violent acts including starvation, beatings and other forms of torture. Consider Chitra's life: she married outside of her caste but said that she was happy with her choice. Her life was harmonious, having experienced neither pain nor humiliation from her in-laws. In the same room where I held the interview, an old sad woman addressed a deeper problem. She said, "I want to know what we can do, do not worry about me; I am getting old now. How can our daughters live in peace?" (Old brahman woman Interview 2005). While most in the room did not have the answer to the woman's question, it was clear that it was a question that many mothers had been pondering. Men, the protectors of families, were equally at a loss with regard to this issue. Although they spend inordinate amounts of time in search of the perfect groom for their daughters, they could not offer the protection their girls would need when they moved out of their family home as brides. They realized that setting up women's organizations to monitor and protect families from being pressured to give huge dowry payments did not ultimately guarantee peace and joy for their daughters. Women are increasingly becoming mindful of the violence inflicted upon married girls, or the cases of dowry-related deaths, and also, the remarriages of widowed men. This information is given wide radio and TV coverage, through which these painful stories are narrated. The thought of keeping unmarried daughters at home poses different sorts of problems. With the demise of a girl's parents, her brothers' wives will begin to persecute their unmarried sister-in-law as she is viewed as a burden on the family's resources. Educated married women are not spared the humiliation as they too endure physical and mental torture by their in-laws. A younger married woman reiterated that things were different amongst her generation. She said, "Married young brides will not endure torture from husbands, brothers- or sisters-in-law and will answer back. But we dreaded our in-laws. We were dead scared of all older relatives and couldn't talk back to them. In any case, our mother-in-law often, for no reason, beat us. We used to keep quiet, never had the guts to protest. But now daughters-in-law would beat their mothers-in-law in retaliation. We are hearing that, and it has happened in our area. The mother-in-law is scared stiff, doesn't open her mouth" (Chitra Interview 2005). The discussion of mixed marriages brings into the discourse the idea of freedom to choose a husband. However, there are limitations regarding the choice of a husband. Addressing the issue of inter-caste marriage, a mother pleads with her daughter in order to try and change her decision and convince her that an inter-caste marriage would be damaging to the honor and respect of their family. Yet, the parents fear that by disapproving of their daughters' choices of husbands, they may be subjecting them to psychological torture, which may result in drastic and sometimes tragic actions, such as suicide.

The increase in inter-caste unions where, seemingly, tradition is challenging conventional arranged marriages, confirms what the young girls say. Marriage without dowry is clearly an issue of concern for the present generations, and some of them are aware that their parents are not in a position to pay the dowry that is demanded for them. Increasingly, women are taking it upon themselves to arrange their own marriages, even with men from a scheduled caste or a different religion. They are cognizant of the fact that such acts will lower their status in the eyes of their caste and family, causing them to be hated, marginalized, or made an outcaste, and even result in their being verbally abused in public. In the case of Mrs. Chitra, who married into a lower caste family, her father often publicly lamented her defiance and dishonor, echoing the disgrace she had caused him. Mrs. Chitra insisted that she made the right choice, considering the poor economic status of her father, and her awareness that she could never enter a good marriage without the means to pay a hefty dowry. She stressed, "Had I stuck to the caste priorities, I would never have gotten married. I am happily married. My husband cares for me, fulfills all my needs. Whatever I require he provides. My father would never have been able to arrange my marriage to a good family and an eligible groom within our caste. I don't believe in the caste system. This is my personal affair. No one has any right to interfere" (Chitra Interview 2005). Her father arranged her elder sister's marriage within their caste, but her in-laws tortured her so badly that, finally, unable to bear the physical and mental torture, she returned home with nothing. She never returned to her in-laws' house, and instead, divorced her husband legally. After a short stay with her parents, she later bought land in the outskirts of town where she built the house in which she lives, and has never remarried.[1] Chitra is economically in a position to assist her sister and family, but she cannot extend financial support to her family. "I feel very sad about that. My parent's family treated my husband badly, even insulted him; he was humiliated without any reason. Consumed by his ire, he cannot stand my parents or any other relatives. That is why he is against giving them the slightest economic help. He still harbors that old anger in him and this will never be over" (ibid). And even though her parents passed away, she is still not allowed to visit her ancestral home. This is the case of two sisters experiencing radical differences in their married states. Their stories describe the inability to predict marriage outcomes for any woman.

The mother of a 14-year-old girl begins to worry about her child's future as a married woman as soon as she achieves puberty. Marriage becomes an obsession for the mother, constantly worrying about and searching for a good groom. "She is my only child, so naturally, I have this constant apprehension and thoughts for her to get her married to a decent husband from a good family. Whether my daughter will be able to adjust, deal with everyone amicably, or whether she will be able to perform all her household work properly in her in-law's house, these are worries already; they will not let her be idle and she will have to 'adjust' with them. We may get her married to an eligible groom, a decent family. The boy may have a good job, without any vices, but later he may change into a drunkard, a rude, characterless and spendthrift person. It is not possible to know his character from his appearance; his true character is revealed much later, after the marriage. Therefore, a girl's parents will always have such apprehension and fear" (Sonali Interview 2005).

While most parents are very careful during the groom selection process, they acknowledge that it largely depends on luck and fate to have a favorable marriage in the end. Sonali told me this about the fate of her daughter: "If she is lucky, she will have a happy, peaceful life, and if not, she will face a vale of sorrow. Hindu parents believe that a daughter will enjoy or suffer the amount of joy or sorrow she is destined to have; not more, not less" (ibid). Obviously, no one can alter one's fate, as these women educate me. Many parents cannot afford to give their daughters in marriage with a dowry but when their children take it upon themselves to arrange their own marriage, there is tension between them and their families. In one case, a young woman did not regret marrying an old man. She decided to go against her family ideals of marrying within the bounds of certain castes. Her family terminated their bond with her. This case is repeated in many homes, where some of the broken family bonds are never mended. In a few cases, the ties are restored when one's daughter gives birth to her first child and naturally grandparents are drawn to their grandchild. In Mrs. Chitra's case, she said that her own father took three years to accept her into the family's fold again. They barred her from major Hindu festivals because she married below the acceptable caste status.

Barring sons or daughters from ancestral worship: Its significance to the children

Many couples now face problems with their families due to the nature of their marriage, and more often than not encounter harsh treatment from their parents. A common form of chastisement is to bar a daughter or son from participating in their ancestral worship, and from entering their parental house. For many, choosing to marry out of their caste does not translate into a denial of their religion. They retain their Hindu identity except that they are now outside the fold of their previous caste membership. Before marriage, and the crises caused by the unacceptable partner choice, the families in question are usually friendly to one another, visiting each other's houses, and their children playing together. What causes the sudden change is a marriage that crossed the lines of acceptability, deemed an egregious violation brought about by an inter-caste marriage between their children. In fact, the marriage ends all past friendly relations, setting up a war-like situation in the neighborhood. Rupa, the washerman's daughter, was familiar with her husband—they were neighbors and, in those days, no one talked about the question of caste impurities between the families. Once their love story became public, her parents were under pressure to arrange Rupa's marriage somewhere else, with offers to pay all the marriage expenses. In Chitra's case, a woman from the Dhopa (washerman) caste marrying a man from a scheduled caste, neither partner bothered to discuss the marriage with their respective parents. She says, "On our own, we went to a temple and married after exchanging garlands. He put vermilion in my hair parting; the temple priest married us. The celebrations took place at my in-laws'. My in-laws supported our marriage but my father was against it. The only reason they opposed it was that he belonged to the Moira caste and mine was Dhopa. My family's caste is much higher than my husband's" (Chitra Interview 2005). Chitra's husband, from the scheduled caste, is a college graduate who works as a head clerk in the Revenue Department of West Bengal, earning a decent salary. In age, there is a difference of almost 14 years between husband and wife, but Chitra did not mind. She added, "I married a Moira (a scheduled caste) with my eyes open. I have no regrets whatsoever for marrying him. My husband did not take any dowry, ornaments or gifts from my parents for marrying me. There is presently a dearth of such honest persons without any greed" (ibid). She also says that none of her in-laws' family today works in their caste profession, washing and ironing clothes for others, although their caste name still carries a stigma in society.

In the discussion of unacceptable marriages, different family members with different roles usually raise their concerns about the marriage. These include community members, blood relatives and relatives by marriage. Different forms of punishment surface to threaten future marriages that might replicate such actions of "erring" sisters or brothers. Barring either daughter or son (although it is the general practice that the daughter will take her husband's caste, or religion for non Hindus) from formally taking part in the family's traditional rituals to their ancestors or household deities is painful. Many women referred to this harsh treatment from their parents as regretful. The most difficult is being excluded from the annual autumnal festival of the mother goddess Durga, when all married women return to their father's house to celebrate in the worship. These married daughters have no place to go during Durga's festival, a sad time in their life. Another problem that they would face is being asked to leave their residential place; a son might not be allowed to bring his wife to her rightful home, which is her husband's house. Along the town's margins one finds new settlements of young couples striving to make a home of their own, living a life devoid of kin and caste members because they are forbidden from starting a life in their ancestral home.

Violence, marriage, and the rights of married women

Can married women cut their ties with their in-laws and permanently return to their father's house? What are the options available to them in case they are subjected to physical violence at the hands of their in-laws? Conventionally, a woman's return to her parental house after her marriage remains a sore point and people have assorted opinions regarding this question. Once a woman is married, she will have to take her husband's family name and *gotra*, in accordance with Hindu scriptures. Essentially, she no longer belongs to her parents, and she is expected to abide by her in-laws' rules. To quote Sonali, one of the women I interviewed, "We cannot bring her [married woman] home whenever we want. Her in-laws may not allow us to bring her even if we go there to get her. It falls under their right. This is why it is said that women are others' property, kept as collateral with parents. We bring her up, feed and clothe her, educate her and give her to someone else. We no longer have any rights to her" (Sonali Interview 2005).

The town has few mechanisms to protect women—families seem unable to safeguard a married daughter. There are organizations committed to help women and one of these non-governmental organizations (NGOs) is controlled by the CPI-M (one of the main political parties of the state), but none of the women I interviewed were members. Being simple and ordinary housewives, they were not allowed to take part in processions and protests. But they could join the NGO as members who contribute a minimal fee, and that is interpreted to translate into a show of their responsibility. They did not believe that the NGO could do much to solve women's problems. On the other hand, they recognized that the three major areas that ordinary women needed assistance were in resolving the dowry system, dealing with the torture of women, and addressing concerns about the rape of women. The women felt that the NGO should take bold steps to put an end to and eradicate the practice of these insults on women. They created a slogan reflecting these concerns: *Women will not give dowry, nor get married.* According to one brahman woman, "Torturers of women and rapists must be punished severely. If the NGO can solve these three major root causes of women's demise, common people will certainly trust them. But in reality we can see that the NGO collects the monthly subscription, instead of trying to solve the 'basic problems' of women, I think this committee is just an excuse in Bishnupur" (Old brahman woman Interview 2005).

There is a slightly greater tolerance for inter-caste marriages as compared to inter-religious marriages. Many inter-caste weddings do take place among Hindus in Bishnupur, some of which are negotiated. It would seem that people no longer attach much importance to caste differences, instead they appear to be set on eradicating the caste system while keeping religion intact. Few are surprised at the incidence of inter-caste marriages, as Chitra explains: "If my son wants to have an inter-caste marriage like me I have no objection. But if he wants to marry a Muslim girl, both his father and I and all our relatives will have strong objections. He can marry any Hindu. But my family will not accept his marriage to a girl from any other religion. If he feels compelled to marry he will not be allowed to stay with us. We will not keep any relation with him" (Chitra Interview 2005).

Parents who usually object to inter-caste marriages fear their society's reaction, seeing that the social norms have been challenged. The same society would not take responsibility when an arranged marriage turns out to be violent and abusive. One such example is the case of Chitra, whose story was told by her sister, Meera: "My sister was married to a man from our caste, and many people from our society attended the wedding. But when her in-laws started torturing her horribly, she endured it silently, without protest, never even protested. She was beaten and tortured daily and finally driven out. She came home and never went back. Our society knew about her condition, about the torture and we requested that they act on the abuses. They only feasted at her wedding, but they did not offer to solve the problems. Society has never done anything right for me. I have always been frightened. Our lives have been spent in dread of society" (Meera Interview 2004). But the pressure from one's society is nonetheless strong; people continue to abide by the rules, social norms and restrictions.

Couples who defy family and society, resort to help themselves at times of need. Having dared to take a momentous step to contradict family and caste members, disregarding their decisions and advice, and marrying according to their own wishes, they felt that they were left vulnerable. Many were truly frightened that they would not be able to live in the town or in their neighborhood. They feared being driven out of their *para*, becoming totally marginalized and isolated. To quote Chitra, "If we do not follow their norms they will create problems for us. We won't be allowed to call priests and barbers for auspicious rituals in the house. They won't let us hire laborers for work, nor have servants or maids for doing housework. We have to follow them out of fear. Women are always tortured and imposed upon whether in their parents' house or by in-laws because they are unemployed. Women endure whatever they face because of their dependency" (Chitra Interview 2005). The younger generation dares to love outside the bounds permissible to them, beyond the controlled boundaries where tradition, religion and caste merge in an accepted space with an appropriate code of conduct.

Meenu, a woman from the Sankhari family (conch shell makers' caste) married a scheduled caste person, from the oil producing caste, considerably lower than her caste standing. Her husband did not work in his caste-related profession anymore because of an acquired formal education and an opportunity to have choices for jobs outside of his caste profession. Hers was an inter-caste marriage, but one that was welcomed by her family. Her husband was viewed as an OBC (Other Backward Class), a Kolu (oil producer caste) whose caste-determined profession no longer existed due to industrialization and mechanical oil mills.

She met her husband in college where they were attracted to each other and his mother had always wanted a working daughter-in-law. Seeing that there was no objection from his mother, they married, despite her own mother's opposition. On her side of the family, it was her uncle, her mother's brother, who welcomed the idea of the marriage and helped to arrange it. Her marriage is inter-caste, which she defines as a "love" and a "civil" marriage. She said, "You can call it a 'love marriage' or a 'civil marriage'. We didn't take a hasty decision, to go and exchange garlands at any temple in Bishnupur. We didn't go to court to have a 'registered' marriage. Our families met and negotiated and fixed a date. Therefore, you can call it a 'negotiated love and civil marriage'. We were married formally with rituals. My mother-in-law had wanted a ceremonial wedding" (Meenu Interview 2006)

This couple experienced none of the friction or opposition from their families that other couples in similar situations experience. With the exception of her mother, who harbored some reservations about the marriage, the rest of the family was positive in their reception of the union. Her mother was concerned about marriages that cross the caste barriers, eroding the lines of hierarchy. In Meenu's words: "In those days there used to be some 'caste bar'. My mother's parental family is quite superior; very educated; extremely knowledgeable. She comes from a very 'cultured family', whereas my marital family has no culture" (ibid). The marriage took place and 500 people were invited to the inter-caste wedding. While it was inevitable that people talked about the nature of their inter-caste union, the gossip eventually stopped because of what she was providing to the community. She tutored and gave music lessons to the children in her neighborhood for free. She said, "Suddenly I was the center of attraction in my area, and loved by the local people. That is why they didn't criticize my inter-caste marriage. Some elders may have criticized. My married life is very successful. I am happy with my husband, son and daughter" (ibid). Her husband did not request any dowry from her family, yet her family did give their daughter assorted gifts and kept up with the gift giving during specific life cycle rites for the grandchildren.

She was lucky not to have any sisters-in-law, which made her a special person in her new home. She was employed when she got married, enhancing her position in her in-laws' house. She used her salary to buy the family gifts and whatever else they needed. She said, "My mother-in-law treated me as her own daughter. She would lavish me with love. I don't think I have received so much affection from my own mother even. Of course my own mother loved me, but I used to be really scared of her, so much so that I wasn't able to gauge her love. She had a very strong personality; a very serious lady. I was too scared of her, and it seems that I enjoyed myself more after my marriage (*often the reverse of what one hears*)" (ibid). Meenu's case is unique, in that she felt liberated in her marital home, and her mother-in-law is more of a friend. She had to terminate her employment when her mother-in-law died and she no longer had somebody to help her manage her house and child. The household chores along with the cattle they owned left her no choice but to relinquish her teaching job.

As a mother she had no alternative, because taking care of her son came first. She ran the household on her own until her new sisters-in-law came to live with her in their husband's home. Along with her husband and children, she chose to move out of the ancestral home and give up their share of the joint property to her husband's two brothers.

Asking her how life would have turned out if she had married within her own caste, she replied, "Had I married a person from my own caste, the ceremony would have been 'comparatively better'. My family has a tradition of opulence and a 'cultural function' at weddings. As I had an inter-caste marriage, there was no musical performance. Not even songs on the wedding night. My husband went as a groom, married me and brought me home. There were no cultural festivities, some of which are common in weddings in my family. It was a very simple affair minus any frills" (ibid). At the time of her marriage, the economic condition of her own family was rather poor. She was supporting her sister's four children and her mother, so they were not happy when she married against their wishes. But she kept up the financial support to her parental family.

Old women offered their negative opinions regarding love marriages; those unions end up badly and women lose out. There is a common belief that men are not committed to marriage and they would terminate their relationships with women when the issue of marriage arose. Often a young girl would divulge to me that she had entered into sexual relations with the man that she married later, and that the sexual relation was instigated out of love. There is a commonly held belief that men use a young girl and then give her up for another girl without marrying either of them. The concern here was the future of the girls who were "used" and led astray by such men. The intent of this gossip and stories is to inform me that though some men are honorable, the fact remains that women do not have any value in their society.

The right to choose: Is marriage a new form of freedom?

The caste system has undergone drastic changes, but marriage, considered to be the stronghold of the Hindu rituals regarding life cycle rites, was the last ritual to change within the Hindu social structure. Interestingly, the question of women's status and the payment of dowry caused the change. My recent research project addressed the changes that transpired in the town of Bishnupur over the last thirty years. What I found out is a transformed town with stark and astounding conclusions. I would not have predicted the changes, particularly those that have benefited women while applauding the tradition of dowry. Superficially, it seems that women are offered two ways to address their lives: one, to follow the strictures of the family and continue in the footsteps of the arranged marriage given with a dowry, or two, to select a husband and proceed with one's choice against the rules of marriage. The continuing increase of inter-caste and inter-religious marriages begs the question if the practiced traditional Hindu social structure rests on contradicting and conflicting principles? Upper and lower castes are implicated in the marriage changes facing their societies.

A question that kept cropping up concerned the cultural space and kinship domain of the children born to parents belonging to two different castes, beyond the bounds of culturally accepted union (same caste and/or same religion). Even inter-caste marriages within the lower castes (i.e. Bauri with Lohar) caused a stir. Families within two different yet similar lower castes are equally unhappy about the marriage, just as families from drastically different castes are, although the arguments amongst the respective families may be different in nature. I will return to this discussion later.

Lower castes tend to give their daughters in marriage soon after puberty, at the age of 13 or thereabouts. Giving a girl in marriage well after she has achieved puberty becomes a problem because it will be difficult for them to be accepted by families that are looking for brides. In my discussions with some lower-caste women, I was surprised at the prevalence of both love and inter-caste marriages in their community. In fact, inter-caste marriages seem to be on the increase as impoverished and unemployed women from upper castes tend to marry lower-caste men, and the women from such unions go to live with their husbands and in-laws in their (husbands') community. Some women, such as Meera below, note, "These are 'love marriages'—boys and girls from different castes fall in love and go to the temple to get married. Most 'inter-caste or love marriages' are celebrated outside the homes of either bride or groom. The couple goes to a Hindu temple to get married by exchanging garlands in front of a Hindu deity serving as their witness" (Meera Interview 2004). The parents of the men and women who have entered into an inter-caste union would, in turn, bar them from returning to their familial homes. The couple is publicly shunned and kept away from their immediate family members, strictly for appearances, even though, eventually, the community, their caste, and the groom's family would accept them.

In most cases, the *para* (neighborhood) members (the groom's side) verbally abuse the couple; the respective caste-based community is often angry at their marriage. The neighbors blame and humiliate the families and the rest of the community demeans them because they could not arrange a proper marriage. The couple does not receive any gifts or presents and there is no expectation of a dowry. Contrary to popular belief, lower castes do object to inter-caste marriages, even if the incoming wife or husband belongs to a higher caste. Collectively, caste members face insults and harsh words from others. The community is apprehensive when an inter-caste marriage takes place between an upper caste and lower caste person. It is confusing because the traditional code of conduct is challenged, which makes the idea of status irrelevant—how should someone of a lower caste behave towards someone of a higher caste and vice versa? Many families and communities refuse to redefine and adjust their kinship and conduct relationships. This issue was discussed many times throughout my field research, in particular when the bride came from a much higher caste. She surrendered her high status and accepted a lower caste identity, while her own family retained their higher caste standing.

Thinking about the subject of marriage and lower caste women, I found that it is men who leave home to marry upper-caste women as compared to women, for the simple reason that the lower castes tend to marry their women soon after puberty, the longer she remains unmarried after puberty the harder it becomes to find her an acceptable groom. The parents of the bride and groom of an inter-caste marriage will bar them from returning to their familial homes, publicly shun the couple and keep them away from contacting their immediate family members, making a point to publicly denounce them. Similar to some of the upper caste cases, the public denouncement of the couple by the parents serves to demonstrate the anger of the families even if it is done purely for public appearances.

The rise in the number of mixed marriages and the repeated use of words such as "rights," "freedom to act accordingly," "my fate" aroused my curiosity, so I conceived of an approach to both instigate and create a venue to comprehend the concept of freedom from the mothers who had children entering a mixed union. Why would a mother break her ties with either a daughter or a son who defied a traditionally arranged marriage? What did breaking the code of their familial and caste culture produce? Banishing a son or daughter is one of the harshest actions a parent could take—so, what do parents aspire to achieve by their actions? Are parents against the freedom of choice that their children practice? I found a number of conflicting ways of thinking and interpretation across the two generations. Younger generations felt empowered once they made their own decision; others felt a sense of freedom by breaking off from the traditions of their forefathers and current members of the community. A young mid-ranking caste woman, Meera, who entered into a mixed marriage with a lower caste man, thoughtfully articulated her view regarding her marriage: "Undertaking a mixed marriage is not accomplished to gain freedom. It is not fated that we do so. In spite of having a great desire (for freedom) we just can't or won't be allowed. We can ask for it (freedom), but won't get it. We can't go anywhere, fearing our husband's anger. We won't get permission" (Meera Interview 2004). In addition, she concludes that her husband is a drunk, to go against his dictates would only aggravate a violent situation. "In an alcoholic stupor, you tell me how can we enjoy any freedom? How can there be any freedom? I am beaten when he is drunk. Can't you understand my position?" (ibid).

Nonetheless, the number of inter-caste marriages is on the rise and one can find them throughout the town. Mixed union couples, along with their children, are embedded in all the neighborhoods. A few are still happy about the choice they made; others are not so sure they made the right choice. Meera, the young married woman with three children, articulated her concerns and doubts about her past decision, saying, "I have made a great mistake by having an inter-caste marriage. I feel that a marriage arranged by one's parents to a groom of their (parents') choice is the best. Initially one can have much pleasure, but later one is never happy. There is a lot of distress. You cannot involve your parents, nor can you depend on them, they will remind me that I entered into an inter-caste marriage of my own choice and they are not responsible for any problem or for any sadness, it is entirely my affair" (ibid).

Having married when she was merely 14 years of age, Meera was incapable of understanding what she had undertaken. In fact, she said that she had no practical sense and felt like she had wasted the earlier part of her life. She said, "I firmly believe that when parents arrange marriages for their children, they look around, discuss, and then select the matches, resulting in married lives which are much happier. The children enjoy peace in their married lives, something I greatly lack" (ibid).

Like many others who followed in her steps, her insecurities about her marriage, in addition to her family's problems, led her to rethink the value of arranged marriages. Having arranged her own marriage, she now felt that she had no inroads back into her own family for support, whereas, under normal circumstances, the family is expected to provide an emotional support system for married women. This young unhappy woman felt imprisoned in her current state, for which she blamed herself and her decisions. Her greatest sadness was the fact that she could not disclose her unhappiness to her family, and she did not visit them daily. Instead of sharing with them her predicaments and sadness, she presented them with the image of a happy, satisfied married woman. Her independent actions had caused her utmost hardship. She would never consider asking for financial support from her parents. She was caught in a bind—on one hand she hid her financial problem because she had her husband's self-respect to consider, and on the other hand, she desperately wanted to confide in her parents about her situation. Disclosing her circumstances to her parents would compromise her husband. She said, "He will be in a false position. I can't accept any help without his knowledge, as that will be dishonorable. My parents will think that he is incapable of running the household and has sent his wife to extract money from her parents" (ibid). She added that in her 14 years of marriage, she had never once visited her parents during Durga Puja, a festival when all married daughters are expected to visit their parental house. Her husband's family did not observe the puja traditions.

Torture and abuse of women: Silence in pain

When married women in inter-caste marriages face abuse, they find it difficult to articulate their problems to anyone because the options for support network for such a woman are limited. First and foremost there are her own parents, whom she is perceived to have disobeyed and refused to accept their advice, who will not offer her support. In case of abuse, a woman would endure the anguish without a word of protest, and tolerate the pain and harassment. If a married woman were to kill herself, the suicide would lead to her husband's arrest on charges of bride killing and torture. Committing suicide, known as *atmahatya* or "self-killing," is commonly seen as a way to end one's subjection to pain and suffering, especially when there are few alternative ways to stop the abuse. The couple's parents, as well as the community, often feel that they did not belong in any self-selective union, as negotiated by the couple. These types of marriages undercut the dowry and the accompanying gifts in-laws receive. The popularity of these types of marriages is based on the absence of dowry. Going outside tradition to have no dowry exchange implies a new form of marriage, where the couples choose each other, bypassing the demands underlying negotiated unions. A bride brings her own self to her husband's residential space with no obligatory gifts and her parents will not send gifts and money for the wedding. As a matter of fact, her parents often times cut their ties with her. Not bringing gifts to the in-laws, in their eyes, is a loss and the bride's own father cannot establish credibility within his daughter's new house. When a girl marries on an impulse, without parental permission, she is not thinking of the traditional pros and cons, and what is compromised by not establishing proper marriage and a system of alliance based on gifts and kinship exchanges.

In connection with a discussion concerning mixed union, women today describe violence and torture occurring between married daughters and their mothers-in-law. When choosing each other to establish a union, a couple is working together on an assumption of equality between them; together they decide to break two different traditions, though within the same religion. The equality between the man and woman ceases to make a difference once the marriage is performed. Soon enough, women will not defy the new order confronting them and instead learn to live within the new limitations that seem to be set in stone. In a worried state, they will not rebuke their husbands to act differently and so cause disruption in the house. In contrast to traditional marriage where a bride follows the cultural dictates of her in-laws, that is not the case for marriages outside the bounds of tradition. Women who deliberately marry against family and caste boundaries find themselves in a newly negotiated cultural and traditional space, having to learn household and family codes of conduct and rules for behavior. Initially, the women may subconsciously believe that they would dictate these rules and regulations but they end up following the husband's caste and family ways of organizing their lives. The woman's marriage is contentious and, by refusing to be part of the long line of generational family lore and history, it has caused problems regarding caste lines and the subsequent break with her ancestral traditions. She has dared to break away from them and now finds that she has to join another family's tradition, unfamiliar and strange to her initially but soon to be her only way for survival.

Women clearly articulate the multiple underlying fears unknown before the marriage but prevalent in situations where the woman is economically dependent on her husband. As Meera comments, "Men know that we are stronger than them, and yet we must listen to our husbands. Women haven't made so much progress yet and I doubt if they will, ever. Women are naturally subservient to their husbands. They are bound to obey the 'order' of their husbands' whether right or wrong. Until the time when women become self-reliant financially, they are bound to depend on their husbands" (Meera Interview 2004). Women's predicaments are clear: marrying against her family's desires and dependent on her husband, the dependence creates subservience and limits women's choices. There was a realization that self-negotiated and arranged marriages carry no guarantees. I came across the case of an elderly woman who was married at 12 years of age into a well-to-do family. When she recounts her life's experience, one sees that little has changed when it comes to marriage. After her marriage to an established rural land-owning family, she encountered extremely harsh treatment from her in-laws. The harassments and constant taunting were hard to bear for the young 12-year-old bride. Her daily suffering, even sixty years ago, proved intolerable for her, and the only option was the one she took. She said, "I got so much ill and inhuman treatment, torture, and impolite behavior from them that I could not express in words . . . I cannot imagine that the aforementioned incident transpired in a reputable and learned family. They were so bad, that not only did they beat me daily, but they caused the loss of one of my fingers" (Bina Interview 2005).

One day, she walked out of her in-laws' house to return to her paternal home. Despite being the only daughter of an established and professional family, and the fact that there were dowry exchanges when she given away for marriage, she was still treated with abuse in her in-laws' house. Obviously, the family's standing in the local society could not prevent violence from occurring. She described her husband as lascivious and a drunkard, who, when he got drunk, would beat her incessantly with a stick. Her father had no qualms in accepting his daughter back home and she lived her life attending to his needs and doing the household chores, while training in music. She did not see herself as a feminist nor had she tried to address this point clearly. Her actions defied her in-laws who had started abusing her immediately after they accepted her as a daughter-in-law. Instead of nurturing and protecting a new member of their kin, her marital family treated her poorly. Her only resolve was to run away and return home, a journey that many married women do not freely endeavor to take. Instead, they remain in their condition and endure the violence quietly. In a woman's life, the journey she takes to her married household and in-laws is done once in her lifetime, a tradition that is challenged today by the younger generation of women. When tradition does not protect women, they take it upon themselves to rectify the injustice.

It has proven to be difficult to gauge which families are reliable enough to send their daughters to them as brides. The problems involved in arranging girls' marriages and complying with dowry demands has caused an increase in the number of inter-caste marriages. To follow in the footsteps of one's family's tradition, search for the perfect groom amongst one's previously established alliance groups, with most of whom marriage exchanges have previously been exchanged, was not a guaranteed solution. Demanding a dowry is not the end of negotiations, neither does it determine with finality the amount of exchanges to be expected between the families. Families set the dowry amount of an unmarried girl and giving the demanded amount will allow the marriage to proceed, but there is no end to demands for further exchanges. If the girl is employed, her family will not worry as much since it would usually be her family that sets the points to be negotiated. The reverse is equally interesting, as working women embrace inter-caste marriages; for them there is neither a question of casteism nor a demand for a dowry. After her wedding, her salary is enjoyed by her husband's family, not her own parents. Interestingly, though her father is not able to demand dowry for his daughter from the groom's family, yet they are assured of her safety. As a "service holder," she receives respect from her in-laws and her husband respects her. In fact, she enjoys a great deal of freedom in her marital home. All of the women I interviewed regarding mixed unions attested to the fact that female service holders do not request a dowry from their prospective husbands, although some addressed the issue of men performing the daily household chores, since the wives are out of the home and in the work force. One woman adds, "I know of a man who is unemployed, his wife is an English teacher in Shibdas High School and in her absence her husband does all the household work, including cooking, cleaning, washing clothes, bringing water. He looks after the children in her absence" (Meera Interview 2004). The employment of wives and simultaneous unemployment of their husbands creates a necessary role reversal.

Understanding the meaning of change: Women's lives then and now

Women are resolute in addressing the changes they have experienced, contrasting those changes with the ones their daughters' experience. Girls are living much better lives than their mothers. The town has changed physically; offering more facilities, better roads, more schools and colleges, running water and electricity. Large markets have sprung up all over the town, and there are now important government offices and a courthouse. The means of travel and road communication are better, medical treatment and hospitals are available. A woman stressed the physical improvements, which did benefit women in general. Bishnupur was more of a village forty years ago, today it is like any other big town and the residents enjoy the new benefits; changes beyond the comprehension for the older generation. There is electricity and the means of communication have improved, children do not have to travel long distances for schooling. Living in the town had proved to be better for education, with about seven educational coaching centers and private tutoring. There are three factors that stand against living in the village: absence of schools, lack of proper communication systems, and poor health infrastructure.

When three elder women in a joint family were asked about their fears before they entered a new household, their husband's house, one answered that, "All of them were unfamiliar faces. I've just had eye contact with my husband at the time of marriage. I did not know him at all" (Old brahman woman Interview 2005). On the other hand, the second respondent, herself a local woman from Bishnupur town, said that she had no problem coming to her in-laws' house. Bishnupur was her parental house and the move did not raise any concern or anxieties. The third woman in the joint household answered differently. She said, "My parental house is in a village. I was apprehensive when I came here with my husband. By apprehension I mean 'what will the people at my in-laws' be like? Will my in-laws be good; will the environment be all right? What will my husband be like? Will he be quiet, unassuming, or bad tempered?' I did have such fears. Every bride is apprehensive about her marital home in the beginning because she has to adjust and accommodate herself to a different environment. Now I do not feel like going to my parents. Having lived in Bishnupur, I no longer feel like visiting the village. We live together in a 'joint family,' we are quite happy here, we have no problems" (Eldest of the three brahman sisters-in-law's Interview 2004). These three sisters-in-law, who in their old age still live in a joint household, agreed that they were lucky to have a simple mother-in-law, one who treated them well and never interfered in any household affairs. They described her as a woman with a sweet disposition, never known to lose her temper, who loved her daughters-in-law like her own children. Such a mother-in-law is exceptional, given the stories one hears about the harsh treatment daughters-in-law experience with their husband's mother. Their household tradition concerning women's code of conduct demands that women cover their heads in the presence of the elders, thus they are not totally devoid of codes of conduct appropriate to married women (see Fruzzetti 1992 and1993 regarding kinship rules and the rituals for behavior). The custom or the tradition of women covering their heads has nothing to do with class or wealth. The youngest of the three sisters-in-law adds "We may be given modern education, may work in offices or courts, but we are still not free from the old habits. Many highly educated women are working in high positions . . . still cover their heads in the presence of their older brother-in-law" (Sonali Interview 2005). A lot has changed with time, but many old customs still prevail. Formerly, it was taboo to speak to one's older brother-in-law, touch him, or utter the names of one's father, mother, or brother-in-law.[2] One cannot utter their husband's name. It was a great sin if the women of the house took the names of their elders.

I asked Sonali if she was afraid of joining her husband's house. She said candidly, "I used to hesitate to do what I wanted. I would be scared, lest I made a mistake and was scolded by my mother-in-law. I always had this apprehension and I was scared to take an independent decision there. Initially, I was a little afraid to do anything independently. If I made any mistake, I was scolded and rebuked. Nevertheless, after spending some time there, when I came to know the attitudes and ways of my mother-in-law and sisters-in-law, I participated in the family work. It was not because I would transgress the rules, I was just frightened" (ibid).

Her only 14-year-old daughter had her own opinion regarding life—her parents desired a better life for their only child because, unlike them, she belonged to a new modern generation. She did not share the same fears her mother experienced; instead, she enjoyed a totally "care-free" life. Her upbringing was full of love and care; she was given freedom of expression. Her mother added, "Her life is better than ours. Before my marriage my parents couldn't fulfill my desires because they were poor. Whatever she wants, clothes or 'cosmetic goods' her father buys for her. He does not let her feel the need. She has no worries. She is engrossed in her studies, not having to bother about what is happening in the house" (ibid). Again and again, I came across the limitless use of the word freedom. Despite the discussion of girls having freedom, there seemed to be limits to its meaning. There was a young woman who would not be allowed to marry a Muslim boy, nor was the idea of an inter-caste marriage tolerated. To the question of inter-caste marriage, her mother concluded, that no one in the family would allow marriage outside of their own caste. "If such a situation occurs, we will try to convince our daughter. We will advise her so that she cancels the idea of an inter-caste marriage. We will also tell her that she will damage the honor of the family by entering into an inter-caste marriage. Her actions would harm her parents' respect, all our relatives, everyone will hate us, and they will not keep a relationship with us. She is our only child. If we do not give permission, she may do something drastic; I mean she may commit suicide. Out of that fear, we will have to allow this inter-caste marriage despite our disapproval. That is why I will not gamble with her life. For these reasons, we will permit her to have an inter-caste marriage (ibid).

Regrets after marriage: Consequences of choices

There were couples who regretted the marriage they had self-selected; most of all they bemoaned their decisions to go against their family, the tradition not to marry outside the bounds of caste and religion. The remorse had to do with the ending of family ties, when they were suddenly cut off from their family because they married without family consent. For many, the ties are never mended, while for others the birth of the first child patches the impediment caused by the marriage. In the case of one such mixed union, Mrs. Sonali said that her own father took three years to accept her in the family's fold again; but she is still barred from participating in her father's ancestral major Hindu festivals. The fact is that many of these families were in poor economic condition and would not have been able to marry off their daughters without paying dowry. This is precisely the reason young girls would take it upon themselves to arrange their own marriage, at times with men from a scheduled caste (lower caste) or from different religions. Knowing the sacrifices they would have to endure and how their families would be affected, they persisted and went through with unacceptable unions. Also, it was not clear that the arranged marriages to one's caste and religion would provide guarantee of happiness for the couple. Educated women were not spared; they too endured physical torture from their in-laws. Keeping unmarried girls at home is equally problematic.

Women are hindered by the tradition that they have imbibed, even though it devalues them. Since childhood, they work towards the ideal model of what society informs and nurtures them to accept and emulate. Girls are trained from a very early age to understand the significance of being a woman and the meaning of marriage. They are neither informed nor educated about the cultural aberrations regarding violence and abuse. The situation of uncertainties and tradition often works against them, with limited protection from family. This condition infects women across classes and religions, pointing to the inability of society to seek solutions to these problems. Older women point out that the root cause of the rise of moral decadence in society and the increase in torture and rape cases among women is the institution of dowry, which though outlawed yet persists under different guises, and makes it impossible for women to be married without a dowry. Wealthy families demand dowries despite their well-off condition. Many cannot argue against this new greed in their society, greed that translates negatively on women as if they are sold like market commodities. At the same time, more wealth does not translate into peace. Although a father paid a hefty dowry for his daughter's marriage to her in-laws who were very wealthy, nonetheless she experienced extreme abuse from them. She reiterated that she was lucky to have escaped from that household, saved from further torture and death. She is aware of what some other brides have gone through in their marriages, being killed for refusing to offer additional dowry. She is familiar with the story of a bride who was murdered by her in-laws; they are in jail awaiting trail. In a second murder case, the bride was poisoned because her father was unable to give the in-laws more money; they too are in jail awaiting their fate The act of retelling such stories reminds her of having escaped similar violence and death.

Barring one's children from their familial home means sending them out, away from the places they shared as children. Some inter-caste couples chose to live alone in a separate residential area where they had no family, friends or acquaintances. For a married woman, a husband's house becomes her real home and her parental home becomes a secondary place where she has no rights. Newly married couples constantly visit both houses, a practice that was absent for many of the inter-caste married couples due to the nature of their marriage. Oftentimes couples are not accommodated within their respective in-laws' house. Loss of one's share in joint property came up in the conversation, and proved to be a problem for those who have shared properties. In the case of Rupa, her in-laws owned land and shops, and were of high standing in the society while she came from a humble background with poor parents, but she and her husband were cut off from their inheritance. Her in-laws thought that she was greedy and had married their son for his money. They were deprived of their share of the wealth, even though her husband rightfully owned a fifth of the property. But the law was in their favor. She says, "My husband is a very gentle person, unlike me, I make trouble. I told him that since they (her in-laws) have never behaved properly with me, why should I give up our share in the family property? It is true that if they had accepted me as a daughter-in-law, I wouldn't have taken a single paisa from them. Since our marriage they have been treating me badly, and did not allow us in the house, made him a pauper, had taken away his shop" (Rupa Interview 2005). At the time of the study, her husband was waiting for his father to pass away to take up the case through the courts and the market counsel. He wanted to give his family a chance to arbitrate and settle his share.

Rupa never considered returning to her family because it is dishonorable for Hindu women to stay at their parental home for a long time. Since they were sent out of her husband's home, and they could not go back to her home, they settled for a new and unfamiliar space to make their home. With no kinship ties, relations, or familiar neighbors, they used whatever means were available to them to establish a home. As a family they now belong to the husband's caste, but as individuals, they have two different caste memberships. Being outcastes, this couple still retains the hope of being reconciled with both of their families. Despite the treatment they receive, couples who have antagonized their families attempt to keep in touch with their ritual observances; in case a family member dies, those who were out-casted and barred from family rituals and festivities, participate in the rites of purification and observe the rites for the dead.

When her mother-in-law was sick in the hospital, Rupa, despite her negative and harsh experience with her in-laws, went to visit her. As a dying woman, her mother-in-law asked Rupa for forgiveness for her deeds and treatment of her. Rupa said, "She wept, holding my hands; she tried to tell me about her suffering. She was eager to talk about her sorrows, but unable to express them. She couldn't speak, only wept. She was trying to tell me that she couldn't do anything anymore. The control of the family had passed on to my eldest brother-in-law" (ibid). The dying woman blessed her estranged daughter-in-law, asked for forgiveness and advised her to live in peace with her husband.[3]

Behavior of young girls, especially if they go against families and caste precepts, reflects the political standing of families in the town. The fear of inter-caste marriages results from the anticipation of being on the receiving end of punishment from their community. Thus, notwithstanding whom one marries, whether it is a person from a different religion or caste, society is neither accommodating them nor willing to accept them openly.

I will now address some of the reasons why families avoid or refuse to accept inter-caste unions even though many families eventually resolve the problems their children created, both for the family and their community. Sometimes the issues created by an inter-caste marriage are even worse than issues from an inter-religious marriage. One woman, who married above her caste rank, concluded that generally society was not concerned with the caste question. They mostly point to women who marry for money, denying that emotions of love could have been a reason for the marriage. Secondly, the next major worry is the offspring of a union between a high and low caste couple, implying that the children will be born of bad moral character. Often, those who are marginalized due to their choices believe that society will take up the cause of and follow those who are wealthy and powerful. Today, in this town, it is not simply a situation of caste difference but also class. Cases of inter-marriages, which have challenged societal acceptability, often occur in unions where girls from poor families marry men below their caste status but with better economic status. Yet, there are cases where arranged marriages fail due to unforeseen situations. At 18 years of age, a young woman's marriage was arranged by her family and Kokila agreed to the match since her family assured her that the groom came from a good family and they were affluent. She said, "I assumed that he must be good but later I found that he was of loose moral character. Amongst his four brothers, it was only my husband who was a drunkard and addicted to prostitutes. My scoundrel husband has abandoned me and married again, even though we are not legally separated. If he hadn't married, my problems would have been more. He would have visited and tortured me both physically and mentally and taken whatever money I had" (Kokila Interview 2005).

Kokila was married according to all of the marriage rites, where her family gave gifts and a dowry. At the marriage reception, friends, neighbors and relatives were invited. Hers was a marriage performed with witnesses, whereas the husband's second, and supposedly love, marriage was conducted in secrecy. Today Kokila lives with her only son, a young man of 27 years who is employed. She gave birth in her parental house and, according to usual custom, her husband should have visited and taken her back to her in-laws' house, but that did not happen. She raised her son alone, making *ghee* (clarified butter) from the milk of her four cows. About her husband she says, "My husband is dead as far as I am concerned. I have never received the slightest love or affection from him. He has remarried and that has been a boon for me. Otherwise the rogue would have troubled and tortured me all my life, or even murdered me. There is no limit to human greed. He would have killed me out of greed for more dowry demands, married other women and ruined her life as well" (ibid). She was convinced that her husband wanted to kill her. He withheld food and clothing from her and made her life miserable with the hope that she might end up killing herself. She said, "He always used to torture me physically and mentally to push me to kill myself. But when he saw that I wouldn't commit suicide, he had planned to murder me. I somehow came to know of his evil plans and escaped to my parents. By then I was pregnant." Of course, Kokila was aware that 30 years ago her parents did not look into the family background of her husband, instead they concentrated on his family's economic standing. They assumed that the groom would be a decent man. She adds, "They ruined my life arranging my wedding with a characterless rogue due to a wrong assumption. These days, parents make inquiries in secret before the marriage and finalize it only if they are satisfied. No parent arranges their daughter's marriage without first finding out the details" (ibid).

About her absconded husband, she adds that it was her decision to separate from him. She was educated and understood what her civil rights were and thus, what was best for her well-being. Being married to him was not a solution. Her sister, who, although not legally married, was in a relationship with a man below her caste status, was not worried that her partner might one day just leave her, given that they had no legal marriage in the eye of society. Kokila asserted that if a woman was competent, her partner would not leave her. By competent she meant the ability to earn and the intelligence to fulfill the responsibilities of the family, to do the accounts of daily expenses and not harm others. She now has a good working relationship and, like her sister, she too has a living-in partner, whom she trusts. She has a successful job and earns a good salary. Her dairy business kept expanding and she had ventured into other business enterprises, all of which were her very own. She launched into real estate business and accommodated boarders in her house. She earned her living through hard physical labor, and her efforts had proved to be a financial success, despite the fact that she was not legally married. The issue here was the independence of women, and whether they rested within a high or lower caste ranking, their employment was always beneficial for them. She goes on to add, "I am telling you real love doesn't exist. It depends on economics. It exists if money is there, not otherwise. As long as money is there, there will not be any want. As soon as there is lack of money love will fly away" (ibid).

I introduced an interesting case, a relationship between two people of different castes choosing not to marry and thus having little interference from their respective families. With one son between them, they could look after his well-being, educate him, and raise him well. Says Kokila again, "I have the capability to earn a salary. He can never leave me for all these reasons. I have a lot of independence here, more than any other married woman. I work tremendously hard from morning till 10 p.m. at night. I make puffed rice (*muri*) and boil grain for rice early in the morning. Then I take care of my ten cows. I cook for the family. Whatever I earn is my own. My husband has no claim on it. No right either. I work so hard, only for love. My 'husband' is very simple and straight. He has never even scolded me. He respects and honors me. In addition, because I belong to a higher caste he is always scared lest I insult him" (ibid). To be insulted or cursed by a person from a higher caste is perceived as a cause for concern for those lower in caste standing. I came across another case where the bride was from a higher caste and her in-laws worried about how they would have to behave towards her; normally a bride lowers herself to her in-laws in deference to the elders, touching their feet. Given her higher caste standing (a brahman), the in-laws had serious fears in this reversal of roles. I will discuss this case in a subsequent chapter.

Returning to the case of Kokila, initially her parents did not accept her "marriage" because her groom was from a lower caste, but later they were reconciled with their daughter's inter-caste marriage as they depended upon her financially and emotionally. Her own marriage was untraditional; her husband took her home and put vermilion on her forehead. None of her in-laws objected to this form of "marriage".

Marrying someone one chooses often causes turmoil within the family, but some of the women are strong enough to bear the consequences. Issues of dowry do not come into the negotiations of these unions, and the marriage rituals are very simple in most cases. Many of the couples that have chosen their partners prefer to live on their own instead of in joint living conditions with the in-laws. Says Kokila, "Here, in my own house I have the right to do what I want provided it is reasonable and correct. I will never do anything that will hamper the respect of my husband. This way we will always trust each other. The kind of happiness and comfort

I enjoy here wouldn't have been possible in my marital home. Women are never able to enjoy much happiness and freedom in their marital homes after marriage (ibid).

It is true, married women are always apprehensive of moving into a new residential space, mostly they fear being abused and victimized. Newspapers daily report stories of women being mentally and physically abused. Often, the women, who are victims of dowry demands, are either murdered or pushed into committing suicide. Married women prefer being close to their parental homes, if circumstances permit.

Conclusion

We are back to the question: Why the rise in inter-caste or inter-religious marriages? Are these a show of liberty from tradition or family choices? According to one of the respondents, "No rules are followed at that moment. People do it out of emotion; they like someone and feel that he is good. They think they will be able to live with him. This feeling of love works" (Meenu Interview 2006). This kind of thinking makes it evident that society is still monitoring and making objections. As daughters of "lines," it is evident that their choices do not guarantee complete happiness. I heard the view "it is my freedom to choose whom I want for a husband" so often that, to me, the word freedom resonated with a totally different meaning. Confusion between what the word means and stands for had led to cases of women who have crossed the lines of acceptable marriages in societal eyes to be extremely traditional and refuse to allow their own children to marry outside the bounds of their caste. Women, who have already angered family and friends, as well as their society, now work to be the ideal wives to their husbands, even if it means reneging on their independence as demonstrated by their decisions to select their own husbands. Meenu's case is one of the successful inter-caste marriages, within which she was employed and managed to support her father's as well as marital households. Although she was financially independent, she had to give up her job in order to fulfill what is expected of her as a mother—to raise her children. She had no support at home to help raise the children and she would not opt for solutions that meant that she would somehow abandon them. She said, "This was my big task, and I had to listen to my husband's logical explanation, although he didn't really put any pressure on me to give up my job. I thought to myself that as a mother, my primary responsibility was to nurture my children and give them a proper education" (Meenu Interview 2006). Interestingly, her son, who was in college, did not want a working mother whereas her daughter chided her for giving up her career.

It is true that women's lives have improved, but all the women agree that it is not enough. Women are better educated, more of them attend schools and colleges; are more liberated; they can travel widely, though they are not allowed out of the house after dark without an escort. Education has helped them to think independently. Compared to forty years ago, today, the rate of education for women is extremely high, more than the numbers for educated men. One finds women employed in various professions— as teachers, government employees, engineers, and doctors, among others. Girls, unlike the past, demand education, with the view that they have a right to learn. The idea of completing one's education comes before thinking of marriage.

Notes

1. Today, she looks after herself by making paper bags at home and sells them to shops. What she earns is sufficient to support both her son and herself. Her sister Chitra covers some of the son's educational expenses. The now young man gives tuition to young school children for his pocket money. Although he has graduated from the local college he is still unemployed.
2. The reference to the brother-in-law, though an old custom, is still observed in some families. These rules are applicable in many Bengali middle-class families. However, it is one of those customs that is disappearing.
3. Although she was not asked to attend the funeral services, Rupa kept (ashouch) ritual impurity for 15 days and observed the funeral rites in her house with a brahman priest officiating at the service. During the mourning period, the women of the house did not comb

their hair or wear shoes, they did not use oil, lac dye, or vermilion, and they stopped eating onion, garlic, fish, and meat. They took on a vegetarian diet without turmeric, mustard oil, or salt. It is also a time when no one worshipped the household idols. Every rite was followed according to proper religious procedures, and concurrent to Rupa's mourning, the in-laws also observed the rites in their house with the assistance of a brahman priest.

Converting to Islam: the Difficult Journey of Losing One's Faith to Adopt Another

"It is unfortunate that Muslims ruled India for over 900 years. We are not rulers, but common people." (Hafiz Interview 2004)

Religious boundaries and the question of marriage

As a researcher working with families that are distressed and bemoaning the abductions of their daughters, one realizes the harsh and hateful language that is reminiscent of India's Partition of 1947. Inter-religious unions face excessive and inordinate difficulties, based on the idea that the union itself is symbolic of an impure act that is a violation of marriage. Crossing religious lines and marrying out of one's own religious group implies that a fundamental injustice was caused to the community whose daughter or son married into another religion. Families will publicly condemn the marriage, testify to their anger, and denounce the newly established union. In all of the inter-religious marriages between Hindu women and Muslim men, the Hindu woman ends up converting to the religion of her husband, giving numerical advantage to the Muslim community. In these cases, conversion to Islam is a prerequisite to marriage, as well as a requirement for the couple's peaceful coexistence with members of the Muslim community. While Hindus in Bishnupur view joining a new religion and renouncing Hinduism egregiously, it is particularly most offensive to renounce Hinduism for Islam. The tension arising from marital unions between Hindu women and Muslim men in this region is so deep that it raises questions about the particularities of these two religions. What is it about Hinduism and Islam that makes it unfathomable to accept mixed unions among their members? Is it the nature of religion in Bishnupur, or the local forms of worship that causes this destructive social and cultural divide?

When we speak of communities and society at large, we refer to the unmarked yet existing divisions separating one religious community from the other. In the course of fieldwork, families enlighten the anthropologist where one community resides and how they are separate from the other. In the case of Bishnupur, Hindu families reside in very close proximity with Muslim families. In an attempt to distance themselves from the "other," each community constructs their own "other" in accordance with religious dissimilarity. Historically, the communities have been kept apart, except when each community intentionally invites the participation of neighbors and friends across religious and caste divides. When a couple chooses to secretly marry, and later resurfaces to their respective families as well as the community as a married couple, they are essentially declaring publicly that the union culminated out of their own free choice. Usually, debates and arguments following this kind of marriage are concerned with the self-selection of a marriage partner, devoid of prior consultation with family and community members, and all others concerned in the process of marriage. But more than that, the greater concern is often the fact that in the process of self-selecting a marriage partner, religious lines were crossed.

Principally, it is the society more so than the respective families which views mixed unions as an intolerable act that is an affront to their respective religions. For the couples, one of them, usually the woman, is required to convert to the spouse's religion, even though their marriage union is often consensual. In all of the inter-religious marriages between Hindu women and Muslim men, the Hindu woman not only sacrifices her own beliefs, but she converts to Islam so she can be recognized as a legitimately married woman in the eyes of her husband's society. More often than not, her Hindu community frowns upon her conversion to Islam. I found only three cases where the Hindu wife did not convert to Islam upon marriage, but this particular couple entertained a mixed religious union because of their own religious differences, which stemmed from the historical animosity that followed the creation of Pakistan, carved out of India to accommodate Indian Muslims. For all other mixed religious marriages, the Hindu woman converted and yearned to be accepted within her new Muslim society. The public manifestations of societal displeasure and anger, through the disapproval of inter-religious marriage, reflect the social realties on the ground. Often, couples will claim that society will abide with their choice of marriage partner, but it often seems that their decisions to convert to their spouse's religion is consistent with the disillusionment that is expressed by their communities, neighbors and caste members. How is it, then, that they begin to think along the same hostile ideas that are entertained by the rest of society? Marriage based on personal choice is still met with hostility, with the couples getting constant monitoring and daily censure from the rest of society.

I heard of families that, when faced with their children's untraditional and uncultural decision to enter into an inter-religious marriage union, took the bold step of actually helping to set up the marriage, but only if the respective couples sought prior consent and blessings from the family. As much as the families participated to that extent, they did not publicly admit to their approval of the union lest they are confronted by their extended families and caste membership. While it remains true that the untraditional marriage rites in inter-religious unions challenge the caste system hierarchical status, it is also true that the families, nonetheless, attempt to stay within the limits of their Hindu traditions. Marrying outside of one's religion is viewed as spiteful and the union itself exemplifies intolerance to the extent that family members are unlikely to forgive the couple for their decision. Unlike the visible pretense of families appearing to be angry (a part of the enacted social drama) while privately trying to resolve the inter-caste marriage and its community based problems, inter-religious marriages have fewer redeeming virtues to work with. A young Hindu girl in class 9 met her future Muslim husband in her own neighborhood. Her two older sisters were already married but during her own marriage negotiations to a Hindu man from her own caste, she decided to run away and marry her Muslim husband. Her decision to elope with her Muslim husband angered her family to the extent that they have severed ties with her since 2005. Like others in a similar situation to this couple, they got married in the nearby town of Arambagh and stayed away for one month before returning to Bishnupur. Rania married first in the civil court and a few days later she uttered the *kalma* and converted to Islam so she could be married again in accordance with the Muslim faith. She relinquished her Hindu faith, telling me ". . . it is better to be faithful to a single religion. A person can't survive if she has divided allegiance" (Rania Interview 2006). Rania insisted that she married out of her own choice, and was exercising her personal right to choose whom she wanted to marry. She said: "No, we got married impelled by independent choice and personal right." She was not abducted, contrary to common belief whenever a Hindu girl marries a Muslim. "Our homes were in the same ward of Bishnupur Municipality. I've known him since we were children. We used to meet in secret on my way to school every day. I know music and dance. I'd go to dance in various 'functions' outside Bishnupur. He would take me there on his motor cycle. We fell in love and I married him later in secret without informing my parents" (ibid).

Some couples I interviewed informed me that they had attempted to secure approval from their family and caste members, taking the step to follow the Hindu marriage rites and tradition with all the required Vedic rites.[1] Efforts by the couple to try and accommodate tradition, repealed by their type of marriage, are an attempt to reintegrate back into their society, the Hindu community, despite their new caste status. For the most part, it is the concern for the status of their children's future that gives rise to anger. Seeking acceptance and wanting to be part of their own communities underscores the fear and marginalization and the state of being peripheral in one's own community.

What underlies the problems of inter-religious marriages in rural Bengal? What is the most significant and essential difference, or the problem, in accepting the marriage? What does marriage which bridges religious lines serve or create the opposing groups? Particularly, what does conversion mean to those who lose a Hindu daughter? During my interviews I came across only three marriages in which the women retained their religion. For those who dared to cross the religious lines and marry, their act was a cause for tension and at times caused a breakup of old and established ties between families. A young woman, who did challenge her own community by marrying a Muslim, could recount all the other couples with a similar experience. Although not many girls from her Muslim neighborhood had married Hindu men, she could tell me the names of girls who had done so:

> There are about 10 Hindu men happily married to Muslim women. There are others too, but there has been no problem here regarding this. Similarly, a number of Hindu women have married Muslim men. But I must tell you . . . when a Hindu girl marries a Muslim, her in-laws and other relatives accept her as their daughter-in-law with affection, but a Muslim woman married to a Hindu man is not allowed to live in her marital home as she is not accepted by her in-laws. She is not allowed into the house and lives separately in a rented house. The parents sever all connections with their son. That is why we can rarely find a Muslim daughter-in-law living in her marital home (Samira Interview 2006).

Severance of ties to one's own child is indeed the gravest and most difficult act to take; some fathers disowned their daughter or son if either one of them embarrassed the family by marrying across religious lines. I know of a case where the Muslim man cried every time he remembered what pain he caused his mother by marrying a Hindu girl. Nonetheless, the occurrence of these mixed unions is not abating, and the problem is seen to be tied to the increase in dowry compensation. For both Hindu and Muslim families ". . . because the fathers are unable to arrange proper weddings for their daughters, the girls are selecting their own 'line'. They are getting married to working-class men from whatever caste or community" (Ali Interview 2006). Where religion is concerned, one of the couple tends to convert to their partner's faith, often the woman.

Understanding conversion, conceptualizing loss

Conversion is a serious matter and there is little that can prepare these families to conceptualize their experience and to understand what it means that a daughter is no longer seen as one of their own. Usually, the daughter is socialized and nurtured in the Hindu tradition as disseminated by the great ancestors and forefathers, steeped in the same sense of religious beliefs and rituals. Families question the new identity adopted by their daughter because, in their eyes, religion is what is key in centering and forging one's identity. Converting to a new religion (alien in the eyes of these mothers and fathers) by uttering a string of words, a woman changes her faith. Conversion is hard and painful for families to understand, and no level of explanation satisfies them. The anguish of a daughter changing religion from Hindu to Muslim has no parallel. It would have been comparable to inter-caste marriage, but the latter is considered better since it happens within the same religion. Tensions between the two communities are on the increase due to the national debates and the communal crisis in parts of India. Mumbai and Gujarat are particularly affected since these events invariably affect the local communities, giving rise to further crises and exacerbate the tensions between community members. Marriages between the two communities undoubtedly are a cause for the tensions between involved communities. In one specific case, the local MLA (Member of the Legislative Assembly) was informed of an inter-religious "love" marriage by his elder brother, a Muslim man who married a Hindu woman. He wanted to absolve himself of consequences resulting from the marriage. Rukhsaar (the newly converted Hindu woman) informed me about the conversation between her husband and his brother when he (the brother) heard of the marriage: ". . . he told us 'you have married for love you should take your wife home.' My brother-in-law told him that I was a minor and my relatives might inform the police that Yunus had seduced me and married me illegally. In case it happened, the police would arrest us all" (Rukhsaar Interview 2006).

The family was scared of repercussions and approached the bride's Hindu family to alert them of what their daughter had done. The story develops further in that now mothers of both the Hindu bride and the Muslim groom wanted to have no responsibility towards the marriage, as both communities feared that the marriage would spark Hindu-Muslim protests. The fear was so deeply entrenched that Rukhsaar was unsuccessful in her efforts to convince her new mother-in-law that no violence would erupt as a result of their mixed marriage.

The town of Bishnupur has experienced structural changes in the make-up of its community, some of which have surprised me as an anthropologist working on the subject of marriage and the construction of the person. Surely, the new identities are the cause of the mixed marriages brazenly crossing religious lines and caste boundaries. Muslims are aware of the increasing mixed marriages taking place in the town—almost all are against these inter-religious unions. When I ask during interviews about such marriages, I am often reminded by respondents that in their respective families such unions are neither tolerated nor accepted, while, at the same time, emphasizing the tendency of sons from other families to marry outside their community (here community implying a non Muslim).

> Hindu boys are marrying Muslim girls and Muslim boys are marrying Hindu girls. If the respective families in both communities accept the "inter-religious" marriages, there is no problem, but if the parents do not accept it, the couple will not live with their parents (Salim Interview 2004).

Salim was referring to the case of a Kashmiri Muslim boy from their neighborhood who married a girl from the Kar (a Hindu) caste family almost twenty years ago. The Muslims are currently concerned about the question of the children's identity. Within mixed marriages, the identity of the children creates unending debates within the community, as exemplified by Salim's statement: "If the father is Hindu, the children will be Hindus too, taking the father's caste. If a Muslim man marries a Hindu Bengali woman, she is converted into Islam after reading the *kalma* and her Bengali (Hindu) name is changed. She is given a Muslim name. Her children will be known as Muslims. Now, when a Muslim woman marries a Hindu man, she ceases to be a Muslim, she becomes a Bengali (there is a tendency to perceive 'Bengali' and 'Hindu' interchangeably). Her children will be given the father's identity, so they will be Hindus" (ibid).

It is extremely difficult for Muslim women to marry out of their faith, for they are often ostracized. They are denied access to their community, unable to establish any links with their family or the rest of the Muslim society. If they choose to, their own family could reestablish ties with them, but that is considered a personal matter and the Jamia Islamia (Muslim society) is not obligated to accept them:

> Her children will be known as Hindus, but our Islamic society will not keep any connection either with her or with her Hindu in-laws. But if her parents want to have a relationship with her and maintain visitations, it is their personal choice. But our society will never accept her anymore. In case of a Muslim boy marrying a Hindu, she will have to convert, take a new name, do the "*namaz*"[2] and fast during Ramadan every year. This is the rule. Her children will be considered Muslims. This is the custom in our society (ibid).

Salim goes on to inform me that the Muslim Panchayat refuses to accept Muslim girls marrying Hindu men, whereas the reverse is possible on condition that the girl converts to Islam and follows Muslim precepts. On the other hand, Hindus seem to have equally strong objections to inter-religious marriages, based on the perception of loss, in that by a daughter choosing to marry a Muslim man, she essentially renounces her Hindu religion, family and identity. Similarly, marriages of Muslim men or women outside of their Muslim community are equated with the same antipathy and aversions by the Muslims; for them too a son or daughter is lost forever to the other side, with little possibility of reunion or any abiding relationship. A young girl, barely 17 years, met her Muslim husband and secretly married him. Rania's Hindu community was, and still is, against the marriage. Before the union, the two families had a cordial relationship—Rania's mother-in-law used to go and get her water from Rania's house—but after the marriage, she was asked not to come again because, in the eyes of their Hindu society, the girl's family lost face. On the other hand, Rania said that "Had my father spent Rs 2 lakhs to marry me to another man, I would not have been so happy. I wouldn't have got such a kind mother-in-law" (Rania Interview 2006).

Apparently, there were marriage negotiations going on with a man in Bihar, a neighboring state, to marry Rania, even after her marriage to her Muslim groom. Rania's parents looked for her across town, her new mother-in-law would not bend to pressure, nor was she intimidated by the crowds of Hindu men who came to fetch Rania and have her forcibly remarried to a Hindu man. Rania's family sent men from their locality to the Muslim household, who accused Rania's in-laws of abducting their daughter, and asked to have her back.

"I knew where they (Rania and my son) were but told them I didn't," says Rania's mother-in-law. "One of their leaders hounded me a lot at that time. He kept on saying—'you must know—tell me.' I never told him in spite of knowing. I fought with them very strictly and compelled them to go away. I told them straight that my son didn't kidnap or kill her. They had eloped openly. Everyone was aware of their love affair and witnessed them leaving" (Rania's mother-in-law Interview 2006).

Though the Hindu men left, they returned later in the night and asked for Ghalib's (the groom's) father. They left when they were informed that he was sick and would not go out of the house so late in the night. It was suspected that had Ghalib's father known the whereabouts of the couple, he would have revealed it to the Hindu men. The Muslim women stood firm, determined not to ruin the lives of the couple. Muslims are in the minority in the town, thus the fear of repercussion from the inter-religious marriages is real and of concern to the rest of the Muslim *Jamiat-il-Islam*.

Muslims in Bishnupur: The quiet "outsiders"?

Looking at the town and the various *paras* (neighborhood), we find that Muslims are not a large community, but they are dispersed throughout the town. In 1967–69, when I began my earlier work with Muslims in this area, I sought to understand the meaning of the Muslim identity living as a minority in Bishnupur. Indeed, they had unique historical connections to the local kings and they had a sound role to play in providing particular types of services to the townspeople. At the time of the Partition, and the period following soon after, the importance of the Muslims in the town diminished, in similar fashion as the decline of the relevance of the local king. Occasionally, the question of what the Muslims were doing in Bishnupur would come up, especially when referencing communal crises in the country. Generally, they managed to seek out a living, and with the exception of the Akhunji family, they did not threaten the wealthier Hindu families. Today, they occupy three main residential areas: in Kabaripara, where there are about eight or nine Muslim families, while the rest live predominantly in Sheikhpara and Akhunjipara, where the ancestors of earlier Muslims were brought and settled in the town by the local kings. The largest mosque is in Sheikhpara, and the place where all Muslim festivals take place. There are Muslim families scattered in Sankutala, Katndhar, Nimtala and Mollapara, along with a handful of families who live near the hospital. A new area called Kusumbani on Station Road is also inhabited by a few Muslims who have recently settled there, and where a second mosque has been built to serve these families.

When I asked a professor, who has done an extensive study of the local Muslims, about the seemingly unchanging Muslim neighborhood, he said that the old separation of living quarters for Muslims is still the case today, which is an indication that Muslims still prefer separate communal living in the form of residential *paras*. Contrasting the Hindu and Muslim communities, I would add that the existing outbursts of national anti Muslim feelings create the need for separate *paras* based on religious differences. The animosity which is exhibited in discourses at the national level, particularly when one addresses the rising Muslim fundamentalism (or the comparable politicization of Hinduism), is an indication of the increase of hidden feelings of distrust and suspicion. For a long time, both communities shared in each other's religious and social festivities, in spite of their differences in religious beliefs. But current signs show that the spirit which exemplified communal harmony earlier in the town is fading. Ordinary folks of the town translate the local scene to be evidence of the national political milieu. But a case can be made for the closeness of the lower classes today, as caste barriers increasingly seem to be serving a minor role. Being somewhat better off financially nowadays, lower caste members use their funds to emulate upper caste ways, performing life cycle rituals, with overt pomp and celebration, making a point that they too are able to live like the upper caste. On the other hand, the upper castes are trimming down their public and religious observations due to high costs. Their daughters seem to be moving towards finding their own husbands, and a few have married lower caste men, or an employed Muslim man. Lower caste families adapt upper caste rites by minimizing their folk rituals so as to de-emphasize their lower status. Marrying a higher caste woman enhances their position in society. The case of a Muslim man bringing a Hindu woman into his family and converting her to his religion is reason to brag about the marriage to the townspeople.

Speaking of the history of the town, specifically of the subject of the Muslim community, we can corroborate that the numbers of Muslims have increased, and their economic condition has improved slightly. In the past, many locals left the town for urban areas or to reside in Calcutta. Currently, the reverse is taking place, resulting in growth and expansion of the town. New satellite towns are emerging. Many villagers have bought land and settled permanently in Bishnupur, contributing to the increase of the town's Muslim population. New ideas and challenges appear to have crept into the mindset of the newcomers to the town, as is apparent in the quote below:

> Primarily, Bishnupur was a "poverty stricken area." It used to be so bad that one could find scantily clothed people on the streets. They had extreme poverty written large on their faces. I can still visualize those poor riddled visages. Really, the common people, particularly daily wage earners, were in an appalling economic state. Compared to forty years ago their condition has improved, in particular, the lower castes (Malas Interview 2006).

Historically, the Malabhum kings had employed all of the artisans and some members of the lower castes to serve as fighters in the service of the kings, as part of the royal army, guards, or as armed escorts. After the abolition of the feudal system, the kings lost their power and wealth, and had to release their servicing communities, being unable to provide financial compensation. Many of the lower castes lost their original caste professions and sought alternative work.

A second major and crucial change addresses the residential pattern which, today, does not match the old pattern of caste *paras* (neighborhood). Whereas in the past, people from the same community and profession used to congregate in the same area (e.g. weavers would live in the weaver *para*, blacksmiths in blacksmith *para*, fishermen, Bauris, Khairas, Metes, etc. would all live in their own separate areas), today the population is mixed in many places.

"It is not that others cannot live in Majipara (the blacksmith area)—but they didn't, at least in 1962. People from different communities tended to live in their own caste-based areas and socially associate with each other. That is why we can still identify the *paras* by their old name and profession of the people who inhabited the area" (ibid).

Today the names of the old *para* do not match the status of the residents. Whereas previously upper castes would not live with the lower castes, now they are cohabiting with people from lower castes. Importantly, old caste professions have changed as the economic condition of the assigned caste has improved. Owing to the "seat reservation" for the underprivileged caste, now their children are enjoying the privileges of education in both schools and colleges, and going on to receive preference for jobs in the government. Currently there are many lower caste members who are involved in business, running shops, hotels and restaurants, tea shops, and selling vegetables. Their situation has improved in contrast to the declining condition of the upper castes, because of the economic incentives afforded them by the government. The mindsets of both the upper castes and scheduled castes have changed a great deal. Caste status, which acted as a divider between the different castes, seems to be less of an issue today. However, when the idea of religion, particularly Islam, is factored into the discussion, the divide seems to hold strong.

A parallel translation of caste-based friendly relations is unmistakably absent when Muslims are discussed. The separate communal living is intact—Muslims remain resident in separate residential *paras*. In contrasting the two communities, I would add that the national political spirit, the animosity exhibited in the countrywide discourses, or the rising Muslim fundamentalism on India's borders, all translates into unfriendly ties which underlie and explain the separation and animosity existing between the members of the two communities. In the past, Hindus and Muslims interconnected with each other socially and culturally, the two communities sharing in each other's festivities, both religious and social. The communal harmony exemplified in preceding years has been negatively affected by the influences of public political debates. Malas, a respondent in my research, addressed the idea that the changes that have taken place in the town would affect other social and cultural values of the past. There would be both positive and negative changes, some of which would destroy families, and others, which the youth would welcome. The fact remains that the town is not what it was some 40 years ago. Boys and girls have more chances to interact, whereas in the past there used to be a "closed society," in which people were forced to abide by family and societal rules, and confined within their shared communities. According to him:

> But now, due to work condition, to education, or cultural functions, these new environments bring together boys and girls from different strata of society, different religious beliefs. Some fall in love, and later they get married without the knowledge of their guardians. The situation creates confusion; the youth forget their different communal identities when they decide to get married (Malas Interview 2006).

Although he agrees that inter-caste marriages are very common, Malas claims that the marriages between Hindus and Muslims tend to be rare, and that the Muslim families that are well off tend to discourage such inter-religious marriages. He underplayed marriages between upper caste Hindus with Muslims, making it seem that only members of lower Hindu castes marry Muslims. In my study, it is clear that brahman girls have married Muslim men, and there is a case where an upper caste brahman man married a Christian woman. The absence of public celebrations is not connected to inter-religious marriages alone, but also true for inter-caste marriages. I tried to point out to Malas the misconceptions, clarifying that such marriages were taking place in towns, and were clearly contrary to what he believed to be happening. I pointed out that he needed to know what was taking place and find out the reasons behind the occurrences of these marriages in towns. I found that the mixed unions were neither strange nor unnatural. In any case, I found that the present social environment encourages these marriages. Since the town has changed so much, this crisis is bound to happen. Malas adds, "A relative of mine—the daughter of my brother-in-law (my wife's brother) married a Muslim boy from their neighborhood two years ago. Both of them used to study in Ramananda College. They fell in love and later got married. But she didn't convert. She uses the Hindu symbols used by married Hindu women—the *sankha*, *sindoor*, *loha* and *alta* (lac dye); she has not changed her name or surname, nor has she taken a Muslim name" (ibid).

I knew the family of the young woman that Malas was referring to. I also came to know that her own father disowned her initially, but later, according to Malas, they reconciled and acknowledged her marriage, and have since been privately in contact with the couple. To publicly recognize such a union is believed to be an affront to the community of the girl. Noteworthy to report is the perception that it is most egregious for a girl to convert to Islam. Without being prompted, Malas informed me that all his children had contracted inter-caste marriages, but not inter-religious marriages with Muslims.

Many of the Muslim newcomers were from Marwar and Rajpur, both of which are villages on the outskirts of the town. The rest came from the district headquarter and neighboring villages of Bankura. All of these migrant Muslims did menial jobs, such as operating rickshaws, masonry, working on farms. Unlike other parts of West Bengal, the presence of Muslims in the town is growing, a fact not of concern as yet to the Hindu communities who reside in separate Hindu neighborhoods. Children from all neighborhoods mingle and play together, as well as attend the same schools and colleges. It is through these shared activities and social amenities that, it is believed, young men and women of different religions strengthen their ties and common interests to the extent that they later decide to go as far as getting married secretly and causing tension between the different religions. Usually, tensions arise immediately after the marriage and religious conversion occurs, changing from previously friendly social and neighborly ties, to communal hatred.

Conversions and violations of religious beliefs: Politics of mixed marriages

Communities are cognizant of individual members' infringement of the law pertaining to their beliefs. Muslims recognize that marrying a non-Muslim spouse is unacceptable, and may lead to problems in the marriage. One way that I came to know of such marriages was that different communities brought it to my attention, hoping that I would agree with their opinion of intolerance of such marriages. In addition, individual or group discussions take place within the two communities, further reiterating their religious disposition and discrimination of mixed religious marriage unions. I was asked to ponder over the marriage of a Muslim high school teacher who married an educated Hindu brahman woman, in which case the woman was neither asked nor expected to convert to Islam. This married woman used *sankha*, *sindur* (vermilion), and *alta* (lac dye)—a Hindu custom for married women. Not only did she still follow Hindu traditions, but she also ignored Islamic rules—she did not read the Koran, observe the five daily prayers (*namaz*), or fast during Ramadan. Their marriage offended the local Muslim community, especially when they were seen in public. Their public appearance reminded the Muslims of the forbidden marriage, and fueled their determination not to acknowledge the couple. Their experience was similar to one of a Muslim high school teacher who married a brahman woman 20 years earlier, causing tensions in the town.

Hafiz's ancestral home in Bishnupur is located in Sheikhpara—a predominantly Muslim neighborhood where the oldest and largest Muslim community is located. His family has lived in this neighborhood for nearly seven generations. Both his father and his grandfather were born in Sheikhpara, but he has not kept up his ties with the *para*. Occasionally, if he encountered someone from Sheikhpara in the street, he would converse with them. He assured me that his inter-religious marriage had had no impact on his status, though he chose to reside on the town's outskirt, a space unmarked as yet with religious specification. He could not live in his ancestral home because he was married to a Hindu woman. His ancestral family house and close relatives still live there, but his wife never visited them and he hardly had any contact with his relatives, other than meeting on the streets by chance. His own family members, however, had not commented negatively on his marriage with a brahman. In his own words:

> Actually they like my wife. Those who know me, love me. My brothers' friends visit our house. They both love and respect me. My seniors are affectionate to me. Even though I have married a Hindu woman and not a Muslim girl from my community, no one from the area has ever misbehaved with us (Hafiz Interview 2004).

Over the past thirty years, Hafiz witnessed Bishnupur move away from extreme Muslim conservatism. Previously, the orthodox Muslims would only participate in orthodox and religious customs, and would not associate with people from other communities. In his view, that is no longer true.

> . . . the town loved and respected the Akhunji family, a famous Muslim family of Bishnupur. Akhunji Saheb behaved properly with everyone; gave a lot for charity. He had great mercy for the poor, irrespective of caste or religion. He has donated much of his huge property to poor people to build homes. Most of his friends were Hindus and he visited Hindu homes and ate there

on festive occasions. It was the class element which seems to have resolved the religious differences (ibid).

Intolerance to inter-religious marriages stands in contrast to the seemingly private, benign acceptability of inter-caste marriages. Despite the initial ambivalence to inter-castes unions, it seems that one would rather have one's daughter or son marry another Hindu, despite the caste differences. Hindus harbor the fear of one of their children marrying a Muslim. Seema, a brahman woman who married against her family's desires, states, "We are Hindus. If my daughter wants to marry a Muslim, we have the strongest objections. We are quite naturally opposed to an inter-religious marriage. Since I am a Hindu, my children are also Hindus. I will get my daughter married to a Hindu. I will never marry her to a Christian or a Muslim" (Seema Interview 2004).

She asserted that Hindus would never accept Islam, nor would the Muslims accept Hinduism (though the latter problem is solved through conversion). She claimed that the history between the two religions overshadows any form of endorsement between the two communities. They remain antagonistic towards each other and hostility and animosity surfaces if one challenges the basic belief system of the other. Recently I came across a newspaper article titled "'Love Jihad' racket: VHP, Christian groups find common cause" in *The Times of India*, stating that a religious conversion racket seems to have contributed to the rise in awareness of local conflicting religious groups, where young girls are lured into unions with Muslim men on the pretext of love. As a result, Christian groups along with the VHP (Vishwa Hindu Parishad, a political party dominant in western India) decided to address the problems and deal with the "social evil," afflicting their communities. "'Both Hindu and Christian girls are falling prey to the design. So we are cooperating with the VHP on tackling this. We will work together to whatever extent possible,' adds K.S. Samson, who is involved with a voluntary Kochi-based Christian Association for Action (CASA)" (*The Times of India*, 13 October 2009).

Underlying recent antipathy between Hindus and Muslims is reflected in the nation's politics, which often uses communalism to incite hatred between the two communities. According to Hafiz, a respondent, "Indian politics is now at a stage where political leaders are always trying to create 'communal riots,' trying to sow the seeds of jealousy and mistrust between the communities forever, determined to create discord between the two communities to disturb communal fraternity. Not only Indian political leaders, but foreign powers also try to destroy India's 'communal harmony' and disrupt peace" (Hafiz Interview 2004).

The Muslim high school teacher, who had a strong sense of his town's history, agreed to talk with me about inter-religious marriages and his town's historical changes. Given that he married a brahman woman, and seeing that inter-religious marriages were a topic of discussion in the town, I asked if he thought that the caste system will exist in the next decade or two. Would separate castes be able to maintain their existence? Will Hindus continue to maintain their current religion and caste? I sought to understand from a learned Muslim why is it that, at least in the private spheres, there was acceptability of marriages that crossed religious boundaries, and Hindu women were converting to Islam after marriage.

While Hindu festivals such as Durga Puja, Kali Puja, Saraswati Puja, and Ganesh Puja are celebrated with pomp and public display of wealth, with families spending lakhs to cover the ostentatious spending on the rituals, it is not clear what is happening in the private sphere, especially at a time when religious observations have taken center stage. Indian national politics has shifted towards adopting a non secular approach, as opposed to religious symbolism, which openly uses rhetoric ingrained with Hindu ideals. Hafiz, being more aware of the social environment than most members of his community, wanted to discuss the current "marriage" between politics and religion. He points out that religious fanaticism has become associated with politics since 1990, leaving a tense social environment at the time before Babri Masjid was destroyed. It was within this atmosphere that communal violence between Hindus and Muslims broke out and led to the destruction of Babri Masjid and riots that led to immense disturbance to the lives of both Muslim and Hindu communities. Hafiz and his brahman wife married on July 8, 1992, the same year that Babri Masjid was destroyed. He said, "From my side, by marrying a Hindu brahman woman I wanted to demonstrate that I do not conform to religious fanaticism, I do not believe in any religion prompted by blind superstition. Both of us are from different religious communities. By getting married at that particular time, we have lodged a protest against the wrongdoing of society" (ibid.). His firm conviction to face the consequences that might arise due to his marriage portrayed him as more of an individual and less of a religious ideologue. He was clear that he did not want to be associated with the negative influences of religion in society, and that his marriage clearly demonstrated his beliefs and courage.

Relearning new religious restrictions: The issue of conversion for women

In an interesting case of mixed marriage, a brahman woman married a Muslim mechanic, converted to Islam but was still rejected by her husband's Muslim community. The young couple lived on the outskirts of the town. She and family members knew that she had denounced her brahman caste position and converted to Islam so as to marry her Muslim husband. But it is a known fact that marrying into a Muslim community and converting to Islam does not guarantee a welcome reception into one's in-law's home. I came across a few such cases in the town, in which the woman had gone through the conversion and begun to follow Islamic beliefs and rites, but was still unaccepted in the family.

A Muslim driver/mechanic, employed by a brahman family, fell in love with a young girl, a brahman who was employed in the same family as domestic help. Her employer was her father's brother, and he had given her the job in an effort to assist her impoverished family. The couple secretly got married and chose to deal with the consequences of their marriage later. In many such cases, both inter-caste and inter-religious marriages, the concept of love did come up, but somehow the idea of being in "love" gave the impression of a sordid affair and a disreputable union, far from the traditional perception of love. Shweta and Rahim, who openly identified their union as a "love marriage," were one of the few couples in mixed unions who acknowledged it as such. I found out that many mixed union couples reject identifying "love" as the sole cause cementing their marriage, from fear of the perception that "love" somehow cheapens the union. Rahim and Shweta knew each other for about four years before they decided to get married. Her family lived in Sheikhpara, a predominantly Muslim neighborhood. Rahim was Shweta's grandfather's driver when they met daily and fell in love. None of their family members knew about their intentions to marry as they secretly traveled to a nearby town, Arambagh, where they had a civil court marriage. "We spent a few days with a relative, and then we went to my village to stay at my elder brother's, before we were married a second time. I married my Hindu wife first in the civil court and after that ceremony we were married again according to Islamic rites in the presence of a Maulavi" (Rahim Interview 2006). The Maulavi did not object to marrying them according to Islamic rites, since Shweta agreed to change her religion to Islam and took an affidavit from the court stating that she had changed her name to Shweta Bibi.

Coming back to Hafiz and his wife, both of whom are well educated (holding Masters degree); they do not define their union as a "love marriage": ". . . we married each other consciously as per our wish. We did not have a 'love affair.' We were very good friends. We went to a Marriage Registrar and got married" (Hafiz/ Kamala Interview 2004).

The idea of a civil registered marriage being contrary to a religious marriage did not bother them since Hafiz was brought up in a household that did not observe many of the Muslim religious festivals or rituals. On the other hand, ". . . Hindu puja is observed in my in-laws' house. My mother-in-law is a brahman widow and she observes all the rites. They invite us on all these occasions. We go there with the children. Unless we participate, their festivities are not seen as complete. My mother-in-law is hurt otherwise" (ibid). Rahim and Hafiz do not share the same experience or reactions from their communities. Unlike the case of Hafiz, Rahim's wife had to convert to Islam for her to be accepted by her Muslim in-laws.

Hafiz was concerned about the growing religious fundamentalism and the current state of national politics, adding that religious fundamentalism was sweeping through the uneducated Muslim society, some of who are also economically deprived. He is critical of the growing fundamentalism and has serious concerns with both Hindus and Muslims in general.

> It is not practical to implement the religious prescriptions and taboos of a religion that is 1,400 years old. The present age is that of science. The fundamental orthodoxy of Islam cannot persist now. We have to follow the scientific rules of today (Hafiz Interview 2004).

He pointed to the resistance facing the polio vaccine campaign in the Muslim areas: "If the Muslim community cannot come out of such fundamental orthodoxy, they will never progress" (ibid.). Hafiz is fighting against the widespread illiteracy and poverty that afflicts the Muslim community. He sees that there is minimal to no formal education among Muslim boys and girls in the "interior villages" of West Bengal. Muslim women, who do get the chance to study in primary schools, cut their education short due to pressures from Maulavis (religious leaders) who seem to support the idea that educated women would be less likely to abide with Muslim laws and traditions. As a result, few Muslims work in government positions and the school system of Bishnupur. On the other hand, a Muslim father of three unmarried girls had somewhat different opinions about inter-religious marriages and Islam. He stated that he saw changes in his community regarding marriages, in that girls would not simply accept the choice of a groom for them unless they had prior contact with him before agreeing to the marriage. "In our society, girls are now educated and as a result, quite conscious of their own well-being. In many educated Muslim families we see women meeting the grooms and rejecting them if they do not approve. You can understand that this is the age of educated people. Nowadays, marriages are not entirely dependent on the parental desires" (Salim Interview 2004).

I came across Yusuf Khan who is married to two women, a Muslim widow and a Hindu woman, who each resided in separate houses. His first wife, the Muslim widow, lived in his ancestral house in Akhunjipara, and the new wife, the Hindu woman who had converted to Islam, resided in a rented house in a predominately Muslim area. Yusuf's work took him around the town, visiting many houses, and he thus knows many families. "I am a permanent employee of West Bengal Government land and tax collection department. I firmly believe in destiny. It was my destiny to marry her (the Hindu wife). I also believe in reincarnation. She must have been my friend in my former life. I strongly believe that that is why I married her. For whatever reasons, we are married. I didn't compel my Hindu wife to marry me. She came of her own will. We have a good relationship. There is no doubt about it" (Yusuf Interview 2003).

Their marriage did not bring them harsh treatment from either of their families, and their families continued to relate cordially. Yet, none of the Hindu wife's family members accepted the idea of a marriage involving a Muslim groom. Yusuf adds, ". . . her parents, brothers or sisters didn't want their girl to marry and settle down with a Muslim man. All of them tried to stop it. No Hindu parent in their right mind would accept their daughter marrying a Muslim. They can never accept such a wedding" (ibid). All effort to stop the marriage was unsuccessful, and the couple went through the process of conversion where the Hindu woman took on her new religion after the initial registration of their civil marriage. Yusuf said, "We went to the Kazi and had a registered marriage in Bankura. Our Kazi sahib has the 'power' to 'register' all Islamic marriages in Bankura, Bardhaman and Purulia. He registered our marriage legally. We were married first and then she was converted from Hindu to Muslim. This is the rule of our religion. I had her read the *kalma* and brought her into Islam" (ibid).

The first wife, Fatma, found out about the second wife, after the birth of their first child, while the second wife found out about the first wife after her marriage.[3] Finding out the truth did not change the matter for Yusuf and his second wife. The second wife adds, ". . . I didn't have the remotest idea that he had a separate family, a wife and a child. My husband had kept it a secret; had I known about it, I would never have married him. I already had intimate relations with him before our marriage. I tried to leave him and I regret the terrible mistake I made. I wanted to 'divorce' him but couldn't because I had a soft spot for him and he couldn't leave me as well. That is why I have had to accept spending our married life together like this" (Yusuf's wife, Samia Interview 2003).[4] For twenty years he managed to keep his wives separate. Though his ancestral house had many vacant rooms, the first wife, Fatma, refused to share the house with the second wife.

The question of divorce begins to be a concern especially in some of the inter-religious marriages. For brides who convert to Islam and renounce their father's and ancestral faith, the idea that a divorced Muslim woman might think of returning somewhere familiar or be accommodated back into her Hindu household is difficult to conceptualize. Young brides convert to Islam to join their husband's community and families, but the question of divorce is not addressed at the time of marriage. For some newlyweds, however, the idea of divorce is beginning to be of concern, especially when one spouse converts from their religion to take up that of their spouse. From one interview I came to know of a young Hindu girl who had converted to Islam, and was beginning to worry about divorce and remarriage in her newly accepted religion. Rania's main worries were *talaq* (divorce) or if her husband took another wife. She added sadly that if her husband divorced her, "I don't have a parental home any more. In that case I have no other option but death. I have two choices—to go back to my parents or death. But he won't marry again. In my marital family, my father- or grandfather-in-law hasn't married a second time" (Rania Interview 2006). Her mother-in-law, who accepted Rania in her family, adds that, "I have accepted that my son has married for love. My relatives have commented that if I arranged my son's wedding, I could have received a lot of money. For me, the fact that I have a good daughter-in-law is enough. It is important that my son and daughter-in-law are staying together happily. I have known her since she was a child. A number of people have said that my son is very good. He could have got a lakh as dowry. I have ignored all that" (Rania's mother-in-law Interview 2006).

Many of the girls who marry against the wishes or knowledge of their families do so to avoid the issue of paying dowry. In Rania's case the subject of dowry did not enter the marriage discussions. Her husband, an employed man who would have accrued a hefty dowry had the issue been discussed, skirted discussion of any form of payment by emphasizing that their love for each other was far greater than dowry payments, and a more worthy cause to fight for. Loss of one's faith (the conversion from Hinduism to Islam) warranted consideration of what the woman had to relinquish on getting married and be accepted in a Muslim household. The groom surrendered receiving a dowry from his Hindu wife, while the bride gave up her faith to be fully accepted. In many cases, it emerges that conversion is not enough to guarantee acceptance.

Malini, a respondent, replies to my question whether she regrets getting married and converting to Islam. She says, ". . . I am aware that they (Hindus) criticize me behind my back. Of course I feel sad. But I don't let it weigh me down. My biggest sorrow is that I have never had happiness from my husband since our marriage. He spends most of the year with his first wife, not with me. He lives in that house for months with her. He comes occasionally, gives me the money for household expenses, meets his daughters and goes back. The truth is that my husband's first wife is quarrelsome, shrewd and a vixen. She doesn't want to allow him to interact with me. I must tell you, no married woman would like to share her husband with any other woman" (Malini Interview 2003).

Religious conversion as a result of these new unions accentuates the constant indignation of families who "lose" a daughter. Taking into consideration that traditional marriage would be acceptable only within one's own caste, a Hindu father is also expected to give his daughter in marriage to a groom of the same religion. In a mixed religious marriage, the bride who converts to Islam, in a sense, relinquishes her connections to her father's ancestral lines and family worship. In order to address societal concerns owing to inter-religious marriages, the couple faces challenges regarding marital decisions, and, often, families seriously consider dissolving the ties between the bride and her family.

In mixed religious marriages, the divergent communities' interference cause considerable pain to the couple. The couple spends inordinate amounts of time undoing the problems that arise as a result. The agnostic schoolteacher, Hafiz, described other inter-caste and inter-religious marriages; concluding that many families initially do not accept the unions, and even enact strict measures to ensure that the couple does not relate with their relatives. It is surprising to find that, within a short period, families involved tend not to forgive and forget.[5] Not all couples share similar experiences regarding their "untraditional" marriages; this is the case especially in marriages where a Hindu woman converted to Islam after her marriage to a Muslim man. For Hafiz, who married a brahman woman, his mixed marriage underscores his ultimate beliefs, and he emphasizes that he and his wife had both agreed to marry outside their community. He says, "No one has the right to 'interfere' in our marriage. Both of us thought it over carefully and got married. We thought about everything seriously and decided independently, not compelled or forced by anybody. Our marriage is established on unalloyed and complete trust. No distrust will ever touch our married life. We married with full awareness, anticipating all possible reactions to it. In making the decision, we were not bothered much about the criticisms from both our societies. Nor did we care or give much credence to all this. We don't believe in casteism, and we are free from superstition. We love, respect, and trust each other" (Hafiz Interview 2004). His wife clearly anticipated her community's negative reaction, but she persisted and married in accordance to her choice. They are both educated about what is right and wrong, based on their religious backgrounds, and they resolved to live by their convictions and conscience. They value honesty and good moral character in each other. Their strength helps to guide them through obstacles that may arise from their decisions.

I came across many unions similar to Hafiz and his wife's, but some couples are still not reconciled with their families. In discussing these rather difficult marriages, the teacher is aware of many unions and the couples who have crossed the boundaries of their communities and religions. He is disturbed when he hears of resistance to marriage by family members, particularly in the case of a father who denies his daughter because she married a Muslim neighbor. In such cases, it is common knowledge that the daughter is living in the town, but to her father she is dead, and as such, she is denied access to the family home.

Muslim marriages, dowry, and *mahr*:
Women's challenges and the new discourse

Much has changed in the Muslim society, family and ways of thinking about religion. Although a few households attest to these changes, there are always those who refuse to accept the change. Class and education are two factors that add to how families feel about the town and their communities. Hafiz, the school teacher, comments on the quiet revolt within the Muslim "high families," whose women work in schools, colleges, and offices and earn salaries—which is not commonly accepted amongst middle-class Muslim families. The strong focus on education for girls within the Muslim community invariably affects women and reorients their alignment with Islamic precepts, given that it becomes necessary to work, despite the negative pressures placed upon them by their society. Nonetheless, a working Muslim woman is not absolved of her Islamic practices and the rigid observance of Islamic rules. A few of them serve as the ideal role models within their religious guidelines. A Muslim merchant adds, "If our women follow all the precepts faithfully, love Islam, keep fast, and pray (*namaz*) then our elders, Maulavis (religious leader), will approve of them. They will tell everyone that the women of Kabadipara in Bishnupur are very religious, that they have a lot of faith in Islam. And this will make it easy for our girls to be married into devout Muslim families without dowries. Our girls are married to families who love Islam and they don't demand anything thinking that they won't get such devout girls elsewhere because they like Islam" (Salim Interview 2004). For Salim, it is better to marry their daughters to good Muslim families; and through their good public behavior, acceptable grooms will come forward for them.

It appears that *mahr*[6] has come to be replaced by dowry, adding to problems that Muslim families and unmarried Muslim girls have to deal with. How and when exactly dowry became a concern for the Muslim is not clear. For a Muslim girl to be married, her father has to provide dowry before the marriage is settled. On the other hand, the bride receives a nominal sum promised to her in case of divorce. During interviews with Muslim families, the question of dowry came up. Salim and other Muslims introduced the topic of dowry within Muslim marriages, adding that although it is not a prevalent custom in Islam, being Bengalis, they too have adopted it, and require that no marriage occurs without a dowry. The local Bengali Muslim culture introduced the dowry system, bringing about the changes in the present societal structure. Now, Muslim communities find that they have to offer dowry while considering the marriage of their girls, a practice that was previously considered taboo (*haram*) in the community. Today dowry is an accepted Muslim custom in this area, yet neither conservative nor orthodox Islam, both of which do not recognize the practice, challenges it.

I took note of many changes in the public behavior of Muslim women. One of the most apparent is the use of *burkha* (never used in the last thirty years) when women and girls leave the private sphere to venture out of the house. The *burkha* is a very "costly" item, especially for lower middle-class Muslim families. *Burkhas* are more expensive to tailor compared to ordinary clothes such as blouses or petticoats, kurta, or salwar, but it is preferable to the other clothes for many women. Young unmarried or newly-wed Muslim women are now keeping distance from men who are not Muslim as well as men who are unrelated to them. For the most part, older women are excused from the rule. Young girls, who used to converse and participate in all sorts of festivals and activities outside of their houses, are not seen venturing outside their neighborhood today. Unmarried girls tend to be shy in front of men.[7] Salim, the vegetable merchant, adds, "In the past, our Muslim boys were not educated. Both Bengali Muslims and Hindu boys were not very educated. They were illiterate. Now, people are paying special attention to education of their children. Our girls are passing higher secondary exams and staying at home. Compared to the past, education has spread all over. Boys and girls of our area are now giving much importance to education. And in order to be a member of the society, one has to be educated. This is an accepted norm now, accepted universally" (Salim Interview 2004). Muslims have realized that girls' education today is crucial for their quality of life and that education is not a male privilege. However, an education would not necessarily result in resisting tradition and is deemed to be a good quality to acquire, in addition to good manners, good looks, and good Muslim values.

Accepting the "other" as a bride: Losing families, ties and religion

Many Hindu women who marry into the Muslim community find it imperative to convert to reconcile their actions. Conversion is not a guarantee for acceptance into the new community, for often the bride faces hostilities for the loss of dowry and proper choice of forming alliances with other Muslim families. In a poignant case of a brahman girl who converted to Islam, she was barred from entering her husband's paternal house altogether. Her case is one of extremely sad and painful circumstances. During the interview with the couple, Rahim informed me that his brahman wife converted to Islam so that he could take her home to his family and introduce her to the community. As required by his Muslim faith, she had to follow Islamic rules in the process of marriage. In addition, Islamic rules did not allow her to use the Hindu married symbols to demonstrate that she was married. In his words: "Muslim women don't put on *sankha*, *sindur*, and *alta* (lac dye). My wife is not familiar with the rites of Muslim society. She doesn't know how to do the *namaz*. She is learning our religious rituals and customs at present. She has become a Muslim after our wedding. She is no longer a Hindu. She will not be able to follow any Hindu rite or rituals of worship" (Rahim Interview 2006). The couple could not get married until she converted because he was a practicing Muslim, and he opted to return and live in his *para* (neighborhood). His wife contradicted her husband's dictates, asserting that as long as she was not familiar with all the rules of the Muslim faith, she would continue to act as a married Hindu woman, though she would give up some of these traditions at some point. She adds, "I do not have any knowledge of Islamic rites, so I lead my life like a Hindu woman; now I follow Hindu rites. When I feel within me that I must follow the new religion, I will do it totally. When I am a bit older, I will be more religious, more devout. If I start following religious strictures now, I won't be able to do anything else" (Shweta Bibi Interview 2006).[8]

The vermilion on Shweta's hair parting, a Hindu custom for married women, is very visible. Her husband had put vermilion on her head when they had their civil marriage. She was first married through Hindu marriage ceremonies, as she had not converted to Islam at the time. She later converted to Islam and, as a new Islamic wife, she was expected to uphold her new religious principles and the abiding rules appropriate to Islamic beliefs. The new expectations were instant and proved to be overwhelming for her, as is the case with many other brides who convert. Although she was not expected to practice her old faith as a brahman woman, this young woman felt that she needed time to become conversant with and acquainted to her new faith. Festivals for Kali Puja or Durga Puja are amongst the most important Hindu ritual observations, but Shweta was reluctant about partaking in them. Her husband allowed her to watch the Durga Puja, but she could not pay her respects publicly. After converting to Islam, this former Hindu brahman girl, who was steeped in her religious ancestral household rites, found herself an outsider to all of her past ties to the Hindu community, and felt isolated as a person. Her husband believed that she must be a Muslim, not only on paper, but also in her thoughts and in her actions. She was clearly hesitant to publicly participate in religious practices that she had renounced. To her, acknowledging and assessing her old faith would be tantamount to offending her husband and daughter, who were both Muslims. "That is why, after my marriage, I decided not to offer Hindu prayers. Not that I am really eager to do it. I go to temples, offer obeisance if I feel like it. I eat 'prasad' (sacred food offering) if the priest or a devotee gives it to me. If somebody puts the flowers on my head I accept it with pleasure. I take it with happiness" (ibid).

The pressure about allegiance to a particular faith came from her new religious community, and not as much from her husband, who was a rather tolerant man. She says, "My husband neither puts pressure on me, nor does he stop me from doing anything good. He advises me to choose between right or wrong and lead my own life accordingly. In that respect, he has given me freedom and I don't want to do anything that will harm his name" (ibid).

Regarding the question of residency after joining in a mixed religious marriage, couples frequently had to face the harsh realities that they did not have an assured place to return to after they began their married life together. Regardless of the conversion to Islam for one or both spouses, attempts to follow their religious precepts are met by resistance from family members, who go so far as ejecting them from family premises. The rejection of inter-religious marriages implies that the couples are left to find their own (new) premise, a process which is difficult to navigate. Steadily, the town's map is showing blurred boundaries between the traditional religious-based *paras* that were a core component of defining one's identity. In Bhattacharya *para*, the families are primarily brahmans or Hindus, and the reverse is the case for Sheikhpara where the majority of Muslims reside. Couples of mixed religious unions confront the difficulty of choosing where to take up residency, having often been refused a place in their ancestral house. Parents, as well as community members, use this opportunity to publicly register their objection to the inter-religious marriage, which they perceive as infringement of religious principles and code of conduct. Parents, along with the community, remain strict with regard to what they consider to be egregious behavior by their son/daughter. The religious communities object to providing residence to the couple that enters a mixed union. In many cases, converting to Islam provided no assurance that the family would reconcile with the couple. Rahim's case exemplifies this point: "My mother was sad and upset. She brought me up and I married without letting her know. All mothers have dreams to select a bride for their son's marriage. She did not allow me entry into her house" (Rahim Interview 2006).

As a matter of fact, Rahim was allowed to return home after he sorted out their difficulties, but the living situation proved to be tough. Couples will offer a multitude of reasons as to why they moved out of their ancestral area, most of which allude to the inadequate space and the constant harassment by family members. Moving out of the ancestral home further accentuates the unease in retaining a cordial relationship between the two families. The family of the young brahman woman above—mother and sister—accepted her marriage, and her mother visited her once in her new in-law's house. During the visit, mother and daughter did not discuss her marriage or her conversion to Islam, but she understood that her mother did accept the marriage. Shweta adds, "My mother had nobody else, except my brother. I was her eldest child. During one visit, my mother-in-law disrespected my mother. My mother heard abusive remarks from my husband's mother and she was upset, insulted, and humiliated. Her ill health and suffering caused my mother's untimely death" (Shweta Bibi Interview 2006). Often women who are involved in mixed unions allude to harsh or violent treatment, varying in nature from verbal to physical abuse. Frequently, the psychological effects of these treatments last a long time.

Shweta maintained cordial relations with her Hindu family. She owned joint land holdings with her brothers in her ancestral village. She visited her village with her husband. The kind of disrespect, abuse, and disregard accorded to her by her in-laws were not observed with members of her paternal side. Despite the Hindu commensality rules, she claimed that her Hindu relatives did visit her and shared meals in her house.

Are the choices women make affording them the peace and happiness they desire? By choosing to go against one's family, traditions, religion, and way of life, are these young unmarried girls defying the ultimate odds, given their newfound freedom to act according to their wishes and choices? Can their boldness be measured in terms of the newfound independence? How much freedom do women really have, and do they appraise their defiance in terms of freedom? Do they think about empowerment while undertaking the audacious steps to resist tradition? Muslim and Hindu women give different answers, yet few conceptualize their act as liberating themselves from tradition. For the few women who had courageously discussed the anticipated union with a man from a dissimilar religion and tradition, the sense of courage ended there. They do not feel that they were free, but perhaps daring. In refusing to accept their family's choice of a husband or wife, many were seen to be defiant of their families, anyway. A young Muslim (formerly Hindu) woman's answer to my question about her experience of having selected her own marriage partner was unambiguous. She said ". . . since I have been married, my husband has never treated me badly. He has never tried to stop me from doing what I want. He advises me to act carefully though. My mother in-law does not approve of this type of close relation and that my husband always helps me, encourages me, and cooperates with me. We have peace. He loves me a lot and I am used to doing what I wanted"[9] (ibid).

Abuse and torture of women: The fruit of mixed unions and the "return" question

At present there are many women who continue to suffer after their "untraditional" marriage. Their in-laws torture them, and the rate of abuse against them is quite high in rural West Bengal. Human greed, lust, and desire for a better life have contributed to the increase of women's victimization. The need to get rich overnight, by whatever means, has in many ways influenced the capitalist economy that has swamped Bengali society and communities. Cheating and taking more than one's share in the family's inheritance is evident in recent times, and the squabbles, which take place on daily activities, allude to the disparities of family wealth. Most of those interviewed separately referred to the changes in the society in the context of families, and the individuals within the families tending towards an individualistic and selfish mentality. As a result, joint family systems are breaking up and nuclear families are finding it hard to cope with all of the economic hardships that are emerging. Due to the increase in economic hardships, there is a tendency for increase in the present state of torture of women. Once women are married, their in-laws attempt to extract more money from the women's families by torturing their married daughters, religion notwithstanding. In those cases where no more money is given, the women are tortured both physically and psychologically. The town's people pay attention to the daily news and print media addressing types of abuses women experience. Many women have been reported to have died because of the torture that they endured as a result of their families not having paid dowry for their marriage. Strangely, some of the men insist that this issue is strictly a concern for women, and that it is the women's responsibility to fight against these barbaric acts.

Regardless of whether the marriage is across caste or religious boundaries, torture and violence is an experience that is shared by women. A young Hindu/Muslim family had their experience of suffering. The couple claims they had no regrets about marrying against their families' wishes and across religious lines. There was no glaring "self introspection" concerning their marriage, despite the fact that they are deprived of ancestral property and familial ties. They were ignored when they were sick, and lacked support as they endured suffering in silence. For Shweta, one of the stronger women I met in the study, the verbal and psychological abuse became so unbearable that she could not bear the pain any longer. She went to the police and lodged a complaint against her mother-in-law, who was threatening her life. In spite of living in a rented house far from her mother-in-law, the older woman nonetheless came around, fought with her daughter-in-law and caused trouble. The husband demanded that his wife endure the pain. She says, "Unable to bear the insult, I went to the Bishnupur Police Station at 10 PM and complained against my mother-in-law for torturing me. A woman police officer arrested her, but I felt very bad because I had acted on an impulse and repented. Then I went there in the morning and got her released, now thinking of the consequences of lodging a complaint" (Shweta Bibi Interview 2006). Shweta rescinded her police report and withdrew her case against her mother-in-law. The animosity between the two women was so intense that Shweta felt compelled to leave and find residence away from the family.

Sometimes, Rahim, Shweta's husband, regretted marrying against his mother's wishes, and he wondered what his life would have been like had he married according to his mother's wishes. He said, "I could have seen her loving sweet face all the time. I am staying apart from her, the mother, because of whom I am enjoying the light and air on this earth. I am depressed because of that. She is still alive" (Rahim Interview 2006). He married against his mother's wishes, which deeply upset her because she could have profited from his marriage with a good dowry and gifts. His mother was so angry that she transferred all of their family property to her other sons.

Rahim's case was the first in which I heard a man complain of the pain he was experiencing being cut off from his people. He asserted, "I have to kill myself for the domestic troubles that I am facing. I have no other choice. I have two options. Either I have to leave home or commit suicide, to avoid all this pain. I am living here peacefully with my family. But I am not happy. I have to live here, apart from my mother. That mother who had brought me up with great struggle, who had given me life. I am living here in total sorrow" (ibid). Regardless of Rahim's feelings, his mother did not appreciate that his wife converted from Hindu to Islam in order to appease his family. She continued to torture her daughter-in-law to unbearable levels.

Rahim's mother found reason to fight with his new young bride all the time. She told Shweta, the bride, that she would get her son to divorce her and marry another woman. According to Shweta, "She would tell me, 'Muslims don't rear chicken for love. They nurture them for food. You are being kept here as a chicken. If you cross the limit, I'll put pressure on my son and make him divorce you'" (Shweta Bibi Interview 2006).

Hearing Rahim's side, one cannot ignore the laments the Muslim man utters for having lost the love of his mother. He toys with the idea of going into a second marriage with a Muslim woman, a choice made with the support of his mother and community, so he could regain the lost love of his mother. In the event that such a scenario unfolded, where would his first wife return? What would be the options of these women who converted and lost their familial and religious ties? Is there a space for them to return to their community and family? What had they given up at the time of conversion to Islam?

In the absence of conversion: Comparative cases of Hindu and Christian marriages

When marriages between Christians and Hindus are examined, we find that the unions do not elicit the same kind of hatred and abhorrence that surrounds Muslim marriages with Hindus. Although Bishnupur has a few Christians, there are a number of local tribal communities living in the vicinity of the town who are largely Christian. Of the two marriages I found that involved Hindu men marrying Christian women, both the women were not from the town itself. Interestingly, these two women were highly educated and, at the time of their marriage, were employed. One of the women, who was remarried to a Hindu, claimed that she had not found peace, nor was she reconciled to a married life. Her difficulties with her second husband started with his not acknowledging her existence as a wife, despite that their marriage was not forced. In her view, her husband denied her a child as well. She said that her husband was the sole provider for his younger siblings and old parents, since they were unable to earn a living for themselves. All of them were dependent on him for their food, livelihood, and medical treatment, among other things. He refused to have any children with her because of the pressure to be responsible for the rest of the family. She said, "It is natural for a woman to want to be a mother after marriage. He has deprived me of being one" (Jaya Interview 2006). She confessed that she was forced by her husband to take contraception pills before intercourse for fear of pregnancy.

She continued to inform me about the nature of her society: "Our society is male dominated, women have hardly any rights; especially those women who do not earn. If an 'unemployed' woman acts against her husband, he will immediately ask her to leave him" (ibid). This sad woman had not developed ties with her in-laws, who had essentially barred her from family rituals and festivities, although she lived in the same neighborhood as the rest of the family. She abstained from any visitations with them. "I am a Christian by religion. My husband's caste does not approve of me. They don't like me visiting them, but my husband's brothers and sisters do come to my house. I am upset that I have to live in great hardship, in a dilapidated earthen house. If I speak out, to express my opinions, it will be crossing limits, so I keep quiet" (ibid).

Jaya tolerated the hardships she experiences with her second husband because, according to her understanding of her culture, she did not have other alternatives. Her own brothers lived in the same vicinity and witnessed her unhappiness in her second marriage. They invited her to live with them many times, but she always declined and continued to stay with her husband. After the failure of her first union, she accepted her current husband's proposal, because he was educated and had a good job. Her husband agreed that she could bring her daughter (from the previous marriage) to their new home and together they would raise her. The promise was never actualized—her parents raised the child. In fact, he verbally abused her and tortured her whenever he thought that she was in the way of things he wanted to do. At times, things would get so bad that she left her house and stayed with her married daughter. In her case, roles were reversed, since usually, young married girls facing violence seek refuge in their paternal house. Her married daughter sent her a monthly allowance because she, Jaya, did not receive money from her husband. She says, "My second husband has cheated and betrayed me as well. I have to endure everything under duress" (ibid).

A 62-year-old woman, twice married, Jaya started our conversation by explaining: "I am leading an unhappy existence. Whatever God has fated I'll have to accept. I was born in 1942, during the terrible 'famine'. I was not born under normal circumstances and have had to suffer all my life, since my birth. My life has been a hard one. I have never had any happiness in my life" (ibid). She was serious when she said that her life would be better after her husband dies. Most married women pray to avoid widowhood, and even wish to die before their husbands. In this case, being a widow (which in Christianity does not have the same stigma as Hindus) would end her life of abuse, torture, and pain. She never converted to Hinduism after marriage, and she continues to occasionally attend Christian Sunday service. Jaya's life of tragedy has one cause for happiness—her own daughter and son in-law, who are respectful and assist her often. She attributed her survival on the love that she received from them. Earlier, before her second marriage, she worked in an orphanage where she looked after abandoned children, which suited her well because she had some training in nursing. She said, "My (second) husband wouldn't allow me to continue working. I thought he didn't want his wife to work, so I gave in to him and left my job" (ibid). Being unemployed diminished her independence. In contrast to her unhappiness, her husband did not seem to understand the discomfort that existed in the marriage. According to Jaya, "I have never received happiness from a husband. I am not fated to have it. I do all the housework—cook, draw water, clean, wash clothes, take care of him. He has no problem. He had eye surgery. I took care of him night and day. I try doing the utmost, but he doesn't do a thing, being my husband" (ibid). Jaya was independent and she refused any help from her brothers. Her second marriage was a failure as well, given that her reason to marry was that marriage would provide a way to protect and safeguard her daughter's future. "I feel that I had made a mistake in marrying this man. He has ruined my entire life, he needn't have married me. He had told me that if I can adjust, he would look after us, consider my daughter as his own. It won't matter if we don't have any children. He never fulfilled his duties. He doesn't have a good heart. I did adjust to the marriage, but he reneged the offer to help and to consider my daughter as his own" (ibid).

Interestingly, her own husband acted in ways that marginalized her. She consented to marry him, with the blessing of her father. Both her father and husband negotiated the inter-religious union. Yet, she felt that her marriage was miserable not because of their differences in religious background, but because of her husband's violent nature. She felt helpless and dependent because she did not have a job, as she had given up her job when she got married. She felt that she was in a difficult situation and that her husband was totally in control. She said, "Had I continued to work I would not have been under his control, my condition wouldn't have been so bad. My husband and I could have enjoyed personal freedom. I will have to depend on him all my life. My state is like a caged bird. As long as I live, I will have to exist like this" (ibid).

Speaking to the endurance and her inability to either address or register marital abuse and torture, Jaya used a well known Bengali saying in one of our conversations: "If I spit in the sky it will spatter on me." She was scared of causing a scandal by complaining about the abuse in her marriage, so she decided to remain silent and desist from taking legal action against her husband. Instead she, like many in similar circumstances, endured the pain in her marriage. She blamed herself for allowing her husband to destroy her life.

However, she did not view all men in the same light as she did her husband. For example, her son-in-law proved to be a good man, who was educated, and took care of her daughter. Unlike many other married men, her son-in-law was prepared to have her live with them, but Jaya was "too traditional" to accept the invitation. She was afraid that if she left her husband's house, ill rumors would begin to circulate about her situation. She said, "The local people will blame me and will make allegations that I have left my husband in his old age. There will be scandalous rumors circulating. I have not been able to leave my cruel husband and have endured all the torture (physical and mental) without a word. I have no alternative but to bear everything" (ibid).

She equated herself to many other women enduring similar suffering. In her view, men have traditionally dominated from the beginning, while women have accepted the oppression without questioning the status quo. To counter the situation, Jaya was of the opinion that a woman has rights (and manages to express herself) if she is employed. As such, it was necessary for women to get an education and find employment. In her words, "If women work and stand on their feet, they are self reliant—they will no longer suffer torture and suppression from males. And husbands will not dare to torture wives any more. Because of this fear, husbands don't dare subjugate their working wives. On the contrary, they are scared of her and accord her respect. Now we can see many 'service holder' wives are leaving their husbands and going away. Such incidents are happening here" (ibid). She believed that she gave up her right to speak and her freedom to act when she relinquished her job. In this traditionally male dominated society, women seek self-reliance to earn economic independence. Women must educate themselves, learn profitable work and earn money to improve their condition. Many unfortunate women, who continue to depend on their husbands, suffer silently and endure unfair treatment and torture. She continued, "Yet there are many parents who, despite educating their daughters, are marrying them off with huge dowries (three to four lakhs), and even then they have no peace. The young bride may have to bear harassment, torture, and insult in her marital home. At times the in-laws even murder the girl by burning her or pushing her until she is unable to bear the torture anymore and commits suicide by either consuming poison or hanging herself. This is a regular occurrence, the daily newspaper reports it" (ibid). Jaya's account is true, given the influx of TV programs like "Crime Diary" that show different examples of how women are tortured. Newspapers also report "rape cases" frequently. In these reports, even small girls were not exempt from sexual harassment within their families. Many felt that it had become difficult for women to live.

Trying to understand her fate, Jaya subscribes to the brahman belief that she must have committed sins in her past life and must, therefore, suffer in this world. "What can be done? I am suffering because my deeds were bad in my earlier life. I try to help people selflessly, give them money and food and clothes, share in their suffering, console them, so that I don't have to suffer like this in my next lives. I once read in a Christian holy book—hate sin, but not sinners. This is my chief motto" (ibid). Jaya's father, a brahman, converted to Catholicism and despite the conversion, Jaya thinks of rebirth. Despite being Catholic, she says that she does not want to be reborn in this world again.

In all the cases of mixed religious union, the Christian woman alone did not have to convert to her husband's religion. I did not see any difference for men, in all the cases that I encountered in the study.

Romancing with tribes: Tribal Christian and Hindu marriage

When a high school teacher in Santhal married a brahman man (also a teacher), their story unraveled different explanations about all the things that were considered to be wrong with their union. This was the second inter-religious marriage pertaining to a brahman man marrying a Christian woman in this area. Anand, 38 years, was a teacher in a high school, and his wife, Mary, 34 years, was a mistress in a girls' high school. Mary, a Christian woman from Midnapore District, came to Bishnupur after her marriage. Both Mary and Anand had higher degrees—Mary had her Masters and Anand had completed his Doctorate. Anand's family encouraged the younger generation to complete their education.[10] Looking at Anand's family, we find that all had married well, with spouses who were well placed in society. So what made an educated and employed person to opt for a path which goes against tradition? Is it one's social or economic status that encourages individuals to choose their spouse regardless of traditional opposition?

Anand's wife, the young Santhal woman, who belonged to a scheduled tribe, was an outsider to the town of Bishnupur. Mary, too, came from a family with highly educated people, such as government civil servants and teachers. After her marriage, she chose to change her last name and her children also took their father's religion. Having come from a strong religious background, she also understood the importance of tradition, especially with regards to children borne of mixed religious marriages. Her village of Bhimpur had a number of missionaries and churches and, being a Christian, she was able to study in excellent schools, such as the Christian Missionary School. Despite her marriage to a brahman, Mary continued to attend church services in Bishnupur as, unlike many women in inter-religious marriages had been compelled to do, she had not given up her faith. In her words, "I often go there (the church) to pray. Since I am a Christian, I sometimes participate in the religious activities of the Christian community of Bishnupur and in this church. But when I stay in my parental home, I go to church every day. I go home during Christmas holidays. My husband accompanies me. I observe my own religious rituals. My husband never objects. I have religious freedom" (Mary Interview 2004). Regarding her son, Mary said that although he took his father's (Hindu) name, the parents allowed him to choose what religion he wanted to pursue. She adds, "I am teaching my son how to pray in a church as well as in a temple. We are teaching him the rituals of both religions. We are giving maximum stress on his education. That comes first, then religious rites" (ibid). They understood that religion is a personal choice and should not be forced.

Unlike other mixed unions, this particular couple agreed that their son could choose his own wife outside the faiths of the parents. Anand said, "After coming of age, he can do what he thinks is right. Since we have made an 'inter-caste, inter-religious, inter-community' marriage, he can marry a girl from any religion, any caste, any community. We should not object. He need not know our opinion or even take permission from us. We do not have any prejudice. My personal opinion is that religion is Humanism. I consider every person a human. After having an inter-religious and inter-community marriage, I had family and social problems. I overcame those. My wife stood beside me and helped me to overcome them" (Anand Interview 2004).

Anand and Mary did experience difficulties till a year before the birth of their son. But now, no decision in the household is taken without consultation between the spouses. Their experience saw the elders in the family block and stand against mixed unions. Anand said, "My grandmother belongs to the past, believes in old fashioned theories, rituals, but is also progressive in her ideas and thinking. Being the eldest of the family, my parents could not accept our marriage initially. I married a Christian tribal woman without their permission. My parents, brothers and sister were unhappy and angry with me. My grandmother, who loved me, was able to settle our differences before her death She helped us a lot. She ate food served by my wife, even drank water that she offered her. Normally brahman widows would not take water or food from other castes, but she was not so conservative. She was free from superstition" (ibid).

Nonetheless, members from both communities initially responded negatively. When I asked couples that defied tradition, caste, religion and community, if they thought about the risks they were taking and whether that held any importance or concern towards their actions, the replies varied. There were couples who had not succeeded in resolving the problems that arose from their marriage. Obviously, many did experience hardships and struggles on their own. It was a life lived without the support of their families. As Anand reiterated, they lived through marriage alone, in joy and sorrow. Anand had a unique sense of what marriage meant to him.

He explained to me about the ties between a man and a woman in the following words: "I think being a husband does not mean lording over one's wife. Being a husband means protecting the wife's honor, saving her in distress, to share her joys and sorrows. A husband must always guard his wife. A man or a woman must think very seriously before getting married. And there is something more. If you notice you will see that the future life of men and women depend on their family background and education. The family environment has a tremendous impact on the life of the offspring. Therefore it is very important to have a 'healthy' environment" (ibid). It was clear that not many couples within either arranged or love marriages had this understanding of their union.

Objections to marriages: Going beyond the norm for one's society

Why do parents, families and the larger community intervene in matters of marriages which cross the religious boundaries? What is the main cause for the hostility? It seems that families faced with the marriage of a daughter or son to a partner from a different caste, religion and community, are threatened by the idea that they would have nothing to share with the in-laws in terms of culture and tradition, and as a result, they react with anxiety and negativity towards the couple. In the case of tribal members inter-marrying with Hindu members, religion notwithstanding, the Hindu community members become negative because they are unfamiliar with the culture of the tribal community.

Anand, who was raised conservatively and deeply steeped in his own religion, was from a section of the town known for its annual worship of Durga, the mother goddess. After his 1996 marriage to Mary, they were both barred from visiting Anand's family and attending religious festivities in his home. He explained, "In 1996 I had married Mary out of my own will, without the permission of my parents. They still had a lot of anger and frustration because of it. To be honest, I went through the days of Durga Puja in great sadness. I didn't go out at all. I was very sad. My wife begged me to go out and see the sights. Similarly, in the same year on 25 December she was very sad. Christmas is a great festival for all Christians. Everyone visits family to celebrate but neither of us could do that. She couldn't go that year so she was upset. She consoled me as I consoled her. We had no choice. We belong to different religions but have got married. As a result, our parents were annoyed with us and didn't want to keep any relation" (ibid).

I experienced that in most of these mixed marriages, the women received harsher treatment than men. Often, those who objected were accosted for the breaking of tradition and the defiance which was said to have taken place. Men and women would attack them verbally and in public, taunting the women in such relationships with insinuations that they were seductresses, a title which elicits harsh words and disrespect from the society. Women who defied tradition and religion tended to suffer mental agony and pain. Jaya's case is a good example of a woman who is forced to live in silence, while she is disallowed social interaction with her in-laws. Jaya had suffered severe mental anguish all through her second marriage.

Anand met his wife in a Christian College in Bankura, where he was the college sports teacher. Addressing a question I posed to him about inter-religious marriages, he did not feel that what they did was courageous by any count. He said, "One doesn't get married thinking of society. We got married according to our own thought and choice. When a man and woman become adults and want to have a conjugal life, or want to marry someone, then they think about selecting their 'life partner'. It is the same in the case of arranged marriages as well" (Anand Interview 2004). As a matter of fact, the circumstances differ for different couples and religious backgrounds. Arranged marriages were conducted by adult members of families in inter-community traditional marriages, whereas inter-religious or inter-caste marriages were characterized by self-selected spouses, and issues of tradition were not of key concern. Clearly, there is a rise in inter-caste marriages, due to the growing independence of the youth. Some of the unmarried girls worry about their prospect of marriage. They decide for themselves and enter into unions of their choice, avoiding the problems of dowry and negotiations. Free mixing among contemporary youth is much higher, resulting in love affairs that culminate into marriages later.

Parents' and societal response to violence in marriage

From my observations in this study, I noted that parents were always trying to marry their sons or daughters into good respectable families. Do these marriages always succeed? Given the rise in marital violence, dowry-related deaths, and the increasing cost of dowries, it is not unimportant to ask questions about the outcome of these unions. It is not easy to find a groom who is morally right, living in a good neighborhood, works hard and has a decent job or business and is of good health. Despite this looming difficulty, parents would try to get their daughter married to the most eligible groom from the most decent family in the area. Regardless of investigations to find the best groom, many families tended not to know the true nature of the groom's character until after the marriage took place. Due to some of these oversights, some women's lives were placed in danger, and even resulted in death.

Usually parents would search for the perfect groom—doctors, engineers, and professors in a process that was prolonged to such an extent that, in some cases, the prospective bride became older, and thus became less eligible for marriage. As a result, the dowry demands for such a bride increased and placed the family in an even more difficult position to find a match and negotiate the marriage of their daughter. If they were unable to arrange the marriage with acceptable grooms due to dowry demand, only then would they look for "primary teachers," in which case they would have lowered their standards for the ideal groom. Ultimately, on the basis of her parents' helplessness in finding her a perfect groom, the girl agreed to any groom. Equally, the parents would be relieved from the pressure of having an unwed daughter in the house, and that she would be at least married in accordance with tradition and ritual that is accorded to virgins.

Anand adds, "I have married a tribal Santhal woman who is Christian. I am a Bengali brahman, who is Hindu by religion. In our case, neither religion nor caste was a hindrance. You can understand from our behavior that we don't have any fundamental religious feelings or casteism. Neither of us believes in it. As we don't believe in all this, we have been able to marry despite the differences, and without parental approval. We have adjusted to each other, with complete trust and a sweet, friendly relationship. Our economic condition and level of education is equal, neither is inferior to the other" (Anand Interview 2004).

Interestingly, Anand told me that when he entered into marriage with a tribal woman, he knew that they both shared the same fundamental values which exalted education and work. He said, "If you ask me whether I would have been willing or able to marry an illiterate daily-wage-earning Santhal woman, my answer would have been 'impossible.' My economic and educational standard would not have matched hers, would not be of the same 'level.' The difference would be tremendous. The question here would not be of caste or religion. It is of the difference in 'standard of living, education, culture and economic condition'" (ibid). Of course, given the local town's perceptions of the tribes surrounding the outskirts of Bishnupur, there has always been a fascination for and attraction to the lives of women from the tribes. The idea was to mingle with them sexually but not to enter into marriage. Often, the tribal Santhal women came to the town to sell wood or other items, and their agility, grace, half-clad attractive bodies were hard not to notice. So, when the parents of this brahman school teacher heard about the marriage of their son to a Santhal, a tribal woman, they envisioned him marrying an impoverished woman from a poor/laborer's family. His family was not aware of the changes that had taken place within the tribal communities. Some of these families are affluent and educated, and live in nice houses in clean neighborhoods. Anand said, "I tried to convince my parents but they refused to understand. Later my relationship with them became normal and my parents are pleased by my wife's manners, her education and pleasant behavior. When they learned from her that all her brothers and sisters are highly qualified and her father too was a senior officer in the postal department, they were happy" (ibid). While Anand's family later changed their behavior toward his bride, the same cannot be said for many families, whose attitude and convictions remain unchanged over time.

The act to choose: Confidence or regret for one's choice?

Did Anand and Mary (or the many other young men and women) who opposed "their family's way of doing things" think that they executed an extraordinary act by marrying outside of their accepted communities? Was it difficult and/or comparable to Vidyasagar's effort allowing widows to remarry?[11] Was Anand's marriage an act of courage in marrying a woman from a different caste, community and religion? More critically, was Anand braver than others for marrying a tribal Santhal woman? For Mary and Anand, marriage signifies an interdependent tie, in which the husband and wife depend on each other. They add that being single is viewed as problematic, and if marriage is entered into for sex, that too is problematic. Marriage has its place in one's society, and children from a marriage are accepted, even when all concerned parties do not generally agree upon the marriage. On the subject of unwed mothers, Anand was clear in his beliefs: "A child from an unwed mother is not accepted, it is never possible. In our country, for an unmarried woman to become pregnant is a matter of great shame and condemnation. For fear of public shame, the woman will not be able to leave her room. In case a single woman becomes pregnant, her parents will take her to a nursing home in secret and terminate her pregnancy medically by an experienced doctor. Our society or government does not accept children of unmarried mothers. Therefore it is not possible" (ibid). In Anand's view, a married woman can adopt a child, but she could not bear a child and bring it up on her own as an unwed mother.

Reactions to Anand and Mary's marriage were surprising to them, given that they both grew up in a harmonious family setting. Both of them informed me that they did not recall fights or displays of violence between their parents when they were growing up. Their parents behaved civilly and justly towards each other. Naturally, the two had little reason to think that the world was going to be different and that reactions to their marriage would be hostile. "We grew up in the quiet shelter of home. We are lucky to be the offspring of ideal parents. We were taught not to treat anyone with contempt. To us, our relatives, as well as strangers, are all the same. We do not believe in casteism or religious fundamentalism. We consider everyone to be close to us, irrespective of caste or religion" (Mary Interview 2004).

Anand, on the other hand, confessed that there are times when the two did have "misunderstanding," tensions emerging from their work and life in general. There was also the tension resulting from societal pressures and work life. He said, "Although the mental pressure is responsible for everything, at a later stage I came to feel that I must 'fulfill' the social desires of my wife—provide 'mental support' to her always. This is the main objective in marriage. I must protect my wife in any situation and support her always. I must share her joys and pain. I must be consistent in this. On the other hand, I will expect the same from her" (Anand Interview 2004).

Conclusion

Matters of religion, especially with regard to inter-religious marriage, are proving to be of growing concern. Tensions arise from the perception that a member of the family or community has been "lost" to another religion/community. The implications of this are that the child has gone against tradition and caused the family and community shame and pain. Central to marriages are the enduring bonds children create with other families. In view of the tensions resulting from mixed marriages, we find newer issues emerging that threaten family relations. The issues range from mere hostility between families to permanent termination of family ties and other social relations. Families may as much as sever all physical ties and social recognition of a son or daughter after a union, which is perceived to transgress acceptable traditional and recognizable boundaries.

Notes

1. Vedic rites would include *havan* (fire sacrifice), *saatphera* (seven steps around the sacrificial fire), pronouncing of the wedding *mantras* by a brahman priest among others.

2. The daily Muslim prayers.

3. There is a history behind the first marriage. She had been married earlier, but within a very short time, her husband was murdered. Widowed and with no child, she was eligible for marriage again. Yusuf adds that the widow came for a visit to a relative's home, and one of his uncles asked the bachelor Yusuf if he would consider marrying her. Yusuf had no objection and married her according to Islamic rites. The Kazi married them and they have three daughters, all of whom are adults now.

4. Interestingly, the children of the two marriages are close. They visit each other and often eat together. The first wife accepts and accommodates the girls of the second wife. The second wife tells me a story about the first wife: "She was very ill once, in bed for nearly two months. I had gone there with my daughters then and had looked after her and nursed her back to health. That was the chance to stay together. We would speak to each other. She became well due to my nursing and started fighting with me without the slightest provocation, to make me leave the house. She would abuse me in the filthiest language in front of my husband but he wouldn't protest, just stood there quietly listening to it. He didn't even rebuke her. He is totally henpecked by her. He follows whatever she asks him to do" (Samia Interview 2003).

5. Even the most orthodox families go through this public process, such as the brahman family known in town for their orthodoxy regarding strict observations of diet and behavior. One of the family members made an inter-caste marriage, which was outright rejected. Having married a mid-ranking caste woman, the son of the family lived away from home, and returned to his home after a few years to live there with his wife. Their differences were alleviated and the family accommodated his wife, their daughter-in-law.

6. Muslim bride price given to the bride at the time of marriage.

7. I was told that if a woman has to go outside her *para*, a rickshaw is called for her and both sides of the rickshaw have to be covered with a cloth lest outsiders see her.

8. Although she did convert to Islam for her husband, Shweta still wore the symbols of a married Hindu woman. She wore two white bangles on her hands which, she informed me, look like *sankha*, bangles made of shell that a Hindu married woman would wear. Hers were made of fiber, were white in color, and worn on each hand.

9. Among Muslims, women have to ask the head of the family if they can venture out of the house, and inform them of the reasons for going out.

10. Anand's father was the assistant Accountant at Ramananda College, the local college. His grandfather died while he was studying law, before Anand's father was born. His grandmother was widowed at the age of 17 years. She struggled to raise her son, and was lucky in that she had the support of her parents. She too came from an educated and affluent household. Her brothers were lawyers and doctors and the family's privileged background made it possible for her to care for Anand.

11. Iswar Chandra Vidyasagar was a philosopher and a reformer (1820–1891), who fought for the rights of women in Bengal and India. He was instrumental in establishing widow remarriages in Hindu society.

The Meaning of "Liberty" and "Independence": or the Decision to Choose a Partner

"By liberty I understand it to be the freedom to express my opinion and thoughts to anybody at any time. I should be able to express it. I will not accept or tolerate any 'domination.' I will expect people to accept my opinion. I will not want to live by what others tell me. Then I will expect to work independently. I will act and fight for what I think is right. I will respect my family and their opinions, but if I feel they are blocking my ideas, then I will be compelled to take action" (Young Santhal Girl 2004).[1]

The above statement underscores a young woman's conviction in answering a question I posed to her. Listening to her explanation about the meaning of liberty or freedom, I was overwhelmed by her vocabulary in responding to the issue of women embracing independence and acting on their own. Her emotions reflect the answers I often receive from other young women when the topic of women's freedom of choice comes up. During my field research (2001–2009), I came upon young women who voluntarily introduced select subjects for me to consider in our conversation about the future of their marriage in Bishnupur. Frequently, young women ended these meetings by providing me with information about their own proposed, though contested, choices for partners. It is clear that the girls have an urge to let me know that theirs would be a different marriage from expectation. Taking into consideration my earlier period of research work (1967–69; 1971–73) when I deliberated the question of tradition and life cycle rites, it is not surprising to find the conversation moving to a discussion about inter-caste and inter-religious marriages, unions which were not prevalent in the early seventies or early eighties in the town of Bishnupur. Cognizant of the fact that these emerging marriages are neither tolerated nor accepted by the majority of the families, one ponders as to why they are so widespread. How do families confront or tackle marriage situations instigated by the actions of their children? Non-traditional marriages, and the ensuing consequences of these unions, have to bear hateful and angry reactions from a variety of familial relations living in close proximity, as also from one's own caste members. High school and college graduates fight back against family and tradition, and at times, against religion as well. Their socialization is skewed towards what constitutes an ideal, proper woman. Following a particular culture for women, handed to them by their mothers and women of a line, proves to be ineffective to women who have crossed that line, such as the young generation of high school and college graduates. To them, their life will be significantly different from that of their mothers. Prior to all other expressed apprehensions, the most foreboding model to these young women is to replicate the elders' ways of life in accordance with the specifically approved culture for women and reproduce values inculcated in them as young girls. They seek alternative choices for a husband. Education and earning a livelihood is of utmost significance. The following observation by one of the aspiring young men who married a tribal woman sums up their perception of the new world they want to create for themselves. "Casteism and religion is secondary. At present no one bothers about it. Despite being from different castes and religion, we don't have any 'superiority or inferiority complex.' No racial pride either" (Anand Interview 2004).

How can communities come to terms with these types of problem causing marriages? What compels the young men and women to leap into new ways of living? From where comes the courage to break with tradition, and challenge society? How do they manage to bear the pain of separation from family? Different community members, both Hindus and Muslims, raised a number of unanswered questions; some of which relate to their difficulty in comprehending or finding solutions for the perceived injustice the youth seem to cause the elders. Elders deny the youth the right to choose a partner; on the other hand the youth refuse to follow the tradition of their parents.

The question and the meaning of "liberty" and "independence"

In my investigation of the meaning of liberty and the freedom to choose, I interviewed both married and unmarried women, and sought their views. What is their understanding of "liberty" and the idea of independence to act on their own accord? An educated lower caste woman who married a kayastha (upper caste) man said, "Women are able to make the right choice for their own progress. They don't have to bear the burden of ordinary husbands selected by their parents any longer." She continues, "In India there is no liberty for women. Very few women enjoy personal freedom here" (Piyush Interview 2006).

I found that this woman's particular response explicates a view shared by many women with regard to this issue. Piyush distinguishes between the choice to marry and to follow a life that she will have to embrace despite the difficulties. She is clear that to make one's own choice to marry does not correspond with complete liberty, nor does it guarantee freedom for women. Actually, one comes to understand that these same women who learned to defy tradition did not own their liberties, nor did they enjoy independence to act on their own accord after marriage. Young girls did offer explanations concerning the lack of acceptance of their marriages, and their attempts to justify their actions in the face of mounting opposition against them. Their explanation rests on the idea of having freedom to act in their own right, invariably using these same ideas to explain the decisions they assumed. They assured me that they bear no ill feeling or carry blatant hatred for their parents, but rather that they often make decisions because they lack alternatives to the plans arranged by their parents. Arranged marriages are not endured by this generation, who prefer full control of the choice of their marriage partner. It is not a matter of whether or not their parents can afford the demanded dowry or "expected gift" (as it is referred to today), young girls demand additional information about the prospective groom prior to the arranged marriage discussions. In the early seventies, I conducted research on arranged marriages where I encountered none of the expressed courage to challenge tradition. Today, I reflect and attempt to understand some of these changes concerning the problems families fight against. Generally, the persuasive consensus rests on the answer I often receive from the young girls—the right to make decision that affects them and their future is theirs alone. These justifications or explanations conclude with interjections of having to act freely, with no adult to impinge on their decisions. The word "freedom" tends to carry with it complexities. In particular, there are two words often used to center the discussions on the significance of their decision. Young girls describe their marriage choices as "*amader adhikar*" or "*amader swadhinata*," meaning "our right" and "our freedom," respectively.

Venturing to comprehend mixed marriages and their popularity despite the adversity facing the couples, both young women and men introduced the concept of freedom as having the courage to break the code of conduct and establish a way for themselves. In order to understand what constitutes a "free act" or "the right to act," I pursued further discussions to comprehend what it was that the young men and women aspired to as ideal. Were they seeking to come to terms with the existing limits of freedom? Is their action to be interpreted as a way in search of freedom? Or were they embracing some sort of empowerment? What, in fact, is their understanding and comprehension of being free? Free from what and to what ends?

The idea of "freedom" was often used to describe why one went against the tradition of one's parents, caste and religion, though the word itself is perceived differently for couples. Freedom, "*swadhinata*" would vary in meaning, sometimes staying within its characteristic meaning of being utterly autonomous, or the ability to act out of one's own free will. Freedom would also come to connote different things to women and girls, men and women. For example, it was perceived as freedom if young women were allowed to have male friends visit them at home or they were allowed to talk with men and women friends with no supervision. There are still a number of very conservative families in Bishnupur who would not entertain the idea of boys visiting their daughters at home, even under supervision. With the exception of going to school, girls from such conservative families are not allowed to go outside the periphery of their house unsupervised. The strict supervision of unmarried girls applies to both Muslim and Hindu communities. With regards to Muslim women, they are today required to wear the *hijab* (using a veil to cover their heads), a custom previously not observed in the town.

Without a doubt, to begin to question the significance of the idea of freedom, one has to at least evaluate how it is practiced and what is its usage as an expression. In reality, were these young women free to choose their own mate? Undeniably, they did so, and the act itself created havoc, stress and at times communal tensions (in the case of inter-religious unions). Caste members are known to have raised objections and occasionally have accosted the families in question (particularly where a caste member married outside their caste). Ethnographically, dissecting the concept and meaning of "freedom" or the right to choose carries with it associated taboos. Using the word itself immediately conjures a deviation from the norm. Focusing on what the word freedom means within the context of a traditional society implies leaving the confines of the "accepted" normal family boundaries, the known and familiar nurturing environment. To leave the cultural confines means that one is left open to a social space with no rules or norms for proper code of conduct or decorum. One enters a world with undefined etiquette and modesty; a new society bounded with an environment which is neither a community nor a family unit. For a young woman to denounce the respectability of home, family and relationships which she is socialized into and to choose a negation of these values for an unknown—it is abhorrent for her family to comprehend and to accept. Crossing the boundaries of legitimacy, defined in terms of caste membership and religion, a woman concedes to her right to act upon her free will; here her "freedom" clearly implies the opposite to what she was familiar with or came from. Additionally, her actions contradict her upbringing, values, and belief, which she exchanges for a different world experience. She basically renounces her connectivity to the old world and steps into a new world.

I came to understand that the idea of freedom carries with it multiple meanings. First the rights of women to decide, stated as "*amader adikhar*" or freedom to choose. This does not translate into freedom from tradition per se since most of these couples do end up recreating a kind of tradition for themselves, or in the case of those who convert to a new religion, adopt a new religion and subsequently new traditions. None of the couples that have crossed lines of acceptability thought much about the future of their children. Some had a blurred vision of the future while others were open to experiencing life as it presented itself, and learning from those experiences. Women in mixed marriages had to contend with the question of their children's heritage. A few quickly learned to adjust to the values and traditions of their husbands. Occasionally, I come across a couple that created more conservative and strict rules regarding the future marriages of their children. But what are the mitigating reasons to return to the idea of tradition (*niyom*), even if the concept is redefined, especially after the major dislocation from the familiar to the new and unknown terrain? Inter-caste marriages, though tolerated, are still not the accepted norm.

Did inter-caste marriage or a marriage against one's parental consensus imply a sort of freedom on the part of girls? Is this what they mean by freedom or even liberty, for that matter? If inter-caste marriage or a marriage against one's parental consensus implies a sort of freedom on the part of girls, what exactly does freedom or even liberty mean in these cases? Is it still a free act if some members of the family accept the marriage? When is it truly a free act or a case in which a person acted freely? How do we come to understand freedom when tradition is manipulated and then recreated?

Practically all of the young women who did plan their own marriages had a story to tell and in all of the stories the mention of "freedom" "or liberty to choose" were embedded into the discussion. For many, the idea of paying dowry for their marriage is offensive, given the knowledge that their parents cannot meet the demands of dowry. One young woman told me, "In our country, arranging a marriage for a girl means selling her. Whoever has money is able to get his daughter married. And those who do not, how can they do it?" (Meera Interview 2004).

Deciding to choose a husband in the knowledge that their parents and their in-laws will challenge their choices puts the young brides in a situation that is not always agreeable. After marriage, they come to understand that no matter how free they were to choose a marriage partner, they are now at the mercy of their husband or his family. The original free act to marry against the will of their parents and community works negatively when faced with marital discord. For some of these brides, their acts of freedom in choosing a marriage partner result in a new kind of domination arising from new rules in marriage. The woman in the following quote describes her new life lived with no freedom to act, "It is not fated that we do so (have freedom). In spite of having a great desire for freedom, we just can't or won't be allowed. We can ask for it but won't get it. We can't go anywhere out of fear of our husband's ire. We won't get permission. My husband is a drunk; he will come home and act drunkenly. And if I protest he will torture me inhumanly. You tell me, how can we enjoy any freedom? You won't understand what my sufferings are. How can there be any freedom? He beats me when he is drunk" (ibid).

Lakshmi, a married woman whose marriage was arranged, explains to me that the idea of freedom and what we come to understand by it carries its own limitations. She adds, "It is not good for women to spend much time outside. Nor is it decent. If a woman stays out unnecessarily, or stands and chats on the streets, her neighbors won't approve or will start having doubts about her character; scared of this public criticism women don't spend much time outside and spend most of their days at home. Women shouldn't stay out unnecessarily" (Lakshmi Interview 2005). Meera, who chose to marry her lower caste husband despite her parents' objections, does not consider that she gained any freedom, and in hindsight she regrets what she did. She is aware of her "mistake," and feels that it would have been better had her parents arranged her marriage to a groom of their choice, who would also be from within the caste. Her parents are not involved in her marital discords and will offer neither assistance nor advice at this point. The lesson she learned from her personal experience is not to allow her daughters to marry outside the caste of their father, and that the parents must have the final word about whom their children marry. "I firmly believe that when parents arrange marriages for their children, they look around, discuss and then select the matches. Their (children's) marriages are much happier. The children enjoy peace in their married lives, something I greatly lack. My life would have been happier had I married according to the choice of my parents. They would have had their responsibility towards me. They would have shared my happiness and sorrow" (Meera Interview 2004). Also, she expressed to me that she would be considerate of the age of marriage for her children, for she considers her own relatively early age of marriage as a mistake.

The price of freedom, or the break with tradition, was steep; Meera suffered by her own account. After 14 years of marriage she has not alerted her parents of her anguish and pain: "I have to hide my sadness, put on a false smile and appear before them. In spite of having many problems in my married life I have managed not to let them get even a hint of it. I always appear happy. But it is certainly not true. I am unable to disclose my distress to them" (ibid). Meera avoids further problems knowing the consequences all too well. Certainly she was free to choose her groom, but her freedom after the marriage is curtailed and controlled, something she endures and suffers because of her own choice for a husband. "If I act according to my own desire, not listen to him, do what I want without his permission, he'll 'divorce' me. I am a married woman. I have children and am completely dependent on my husband. If he leaves me now what will happen to me? After he 'divorces' me, no man will marry a mother of three kids. Nobody will take my responsibility. That is why I have to keep quiet. I don't even protest even if he commits a wrong act" (ibid). Her decision is to guide her daughters to think about their self-interest and not be misdirected. She does not wish them to have her experiences.

Once a woman plainly informed me: "This is a society of fear. We are bound by social norms. We are always scared lest people in society criticize us. I may not subscribe to it, but everyone else does. Since I live here (in the town) permanently I have to abide by the rules" (Lakshmi Interview 2005). Notwithstanding any free will in fighting family and community, these women have new worries to reconcile with. They begin to think about the future of their children. Urmila, one of the interviewees, confidently enlightened me that in her own family there have not been any mixed unions, something she is not concerned about since she was sure it would not take place. She adds, "Actually there hasn't been either an inter-caste or an inter-religious marriage in our family so far. Those who are not scared of public shame or dishonor can have such marriages. They do not think of family honor and name. Those who do not have self-respect are not afraid of people's condemnation. Those who are scared of being tortured by their conscience and don't want to hurt their parents and relatives will not have the courage to marry like that. . . . If we condone such a marriage for our daughter, we will be haunted by our conscience. Therefore we will not allow our daughter to have an inter-caste or inter-religious marriage" (Urmila Interview 2004).

One of the earliest women I interviewed, Seema, a brahman who married much below her caste rank, expressed that she did not find her actions to be liberating. She believed that her marriage to a man much lower than her own caste is not an expression of her freedom. Despite her reaction to the idea of freedom, this young woman rejected her parents' negative reaction to her proposed marriage. Her family is amongst the most orthodox families in the town, known for their conservativeness and observance of strict gender rules. Despite her inter-caste marriage, she discovered that her father-in-law observed strict rules as well, and she had to comply with the same restrictions. She was allowed to continue with her music lessons; a teacher was arranged to come to the house to train her under the supervision of her father-in-law. Seema's marriage is perhaps one of the exceptions compared to those of many others who also married against their parents' wishes. Her in-laws were very accommodating, accepting her fully despite their initial objections to the marriage. Seema's true freedom did not imply spending her life the way she wanted. She introduced a new, slightly different meaning to the idea of freedom, adding, "Freedom is spending one's life well, 'freely' is freedom. I am saying I am free in this house because there is no one else here. I am alone. If there was some other person, another brother and his wife, then there could have been a scope for conflict among the wives over small household details, as is common in a joint family. There would have been envy among the women, which is common in Bengali families. There would have been 'friction' about why do I have to do this and not her" (Seema Interview 2004). She defined freedom by the fact that she is alone in the house, and in that sense, she was free of all those who normally would have ordered or dictated to her or limited her actions. Her definition of being free entails the absence of others to dictate to her, she acts on her own within the household, where she is in control of her movements. Of course, she does have to consult her husband if she is to leave the house and the same goes for him. "We do not act impulsively or distractively, in a sense being free does not imply nor is it the same as being willful" (ibid). She agreed that a wild, unprincipled, lifestyle should not be confused with being free. Freedom does not mean doing and acting on one's inclination or impulse. Women whose marriages are arranged by their families confront comparable problems like the ones experienced by women entering marriages that are not arranged. In the case of another woman whose marriage was arranged to a man above her caste, she offered an interesting picture of her seemingly happy life. A talented musician, gifted with a quality which was attractive to her husband's family, she had to relinquish her music lessons and practice. Her conservative family can boast of her talents to others but would not allow her to go out of the house to continue her lessons. The family worries about gossip if she were to go out to the music school to continue her education. "What will others say if his wife goes to learn music and sing at different functions? I have had to stop my music career with a lot of pain and regret for my marital family and my husband. To avoid unpleasantness and to stop our relationship from deteriorating, I have stopped learning new songs and practicing. I obeyed the wishes of my lord, my husband. I had no alternative. After I got married, I used to sit with my harmonium for practice but eventually gave it up" (Lakshmi Interview 2005).

Conflicts with one's parents and community: When tradition is a hindrance

Conducting this research on marriages that were deemed undesirable by the community, I found that the hardest of these were inter-religious unions, especially those cases where the young woman was neither sure nor willing to convert to Islam were particularly problematic (though all those who did convert informed me that they were not coerced to do so). I asked a young woman who converted to Islam and, as a result, could not visit her parental house about her feelings, and she still insisted that her marriage was ". . . definitely for love but also for my right. We got married impelled by independent choice and personal right" (Rania Interview 2006). She is implying that she had the right to choose anyone, even if it meant a Muslim husband. Rania, who began using the new name given to her after conversion, is happy with her mechanic husband and his family, which has fully accepted her as a daughter-in-law.

Comparing Rania's case to that of Rupa's (which I discussed in chapter 2) shows the different reactions of their families to the unplanned marriages. Daughter of a *dhobi* (washerman caste), Rupa married above her status. The union resulted in hostility between their respective families. Trying to avoid anger and surprise, the couple sought permission and/or acceptance from their individual families prior to the marriage, but this was not granted. However, the couple went ahead with the marriage knowing that marrying against their families' wishes could only result in anger. The newly married couple were not allowed to live in the husband's parental place. A married woman belongs to a new set of relations, a husband's house becomes her real home and her parental home becomes a secondary place where she has no rights after marriage. Newly married couples constantly visit both houses; this right was denied Rupa and her husband, who were banned from visiting. Though her own family accepted the marriage, Rupa never considered living in her father's house because it is dishonorable for a married Hindu woman to stay at her parental home for long periods. Faced with these odds resulting from their marriage, they settled for a new unfamiliar space to make their home. Rupa chose her husband who is a Hindu, to whom she is happily married, and tries to raise three daughters within a tight and strict household. But, she informs me, her family would not have been accommodating if she had fallen in love with a Muslim and would have barred them from entering their house, especially if the man was from a lower caste household. Concerning her daughters, she is emphatic that they are not permitted the luxury of choosing to marry a non-Hindu; that she will not accept. "I have strong objections to anyone other than a Hindu marrying my daughters. I can never accept any Muslim boy. This is absurd. Hinduism and Islam are different. There is a heaven and hell difference between the two. Oil and water never mingle. But if my daughters want to do it, there's nothing I can do. But I know my daughters. They will never do something like that. I am educating them properly; I firmly believe that they will never take such a bold step without our knowledge" (Rupa Interview 2005). Considering the antagonism she encountered because of her marriage, she now offers strong objections to any allusion of mixed unions for her daughters.

Surmising why young couples who could go against their society, caste, community, and at times religion still end up succumbing to the stricture of their society, Raj, Lakshmi's husband and father of two girls summed up the matter thus: "There is a huge role of society in our family lives. We can't do anything minus society. Our 'next generation' will follow our footsteps. If I lead a reckless life my 'next generation' will do the same. I will find it difficult to arrange their marriages. People will say 'this man is immoral, a drunkard.' It will be impossible to get them married to decent grooms. Nobody wants to arrange matches with girls from a family of ill repute" (Raj, Lakshmi's husband Interview 2005).

Across class and caste divide, I found many couples that had shared identical reactions to unacceptable marriage proposals coming from their children. In chapter five I take up the issue of mixed marriages and the question of violence. Asking a Hindu girl who fell in love with a Muslim man about her marriage choices, I was immediately reassured that she was fully aware of her actions and had no objections to marrying him. She considered her father's impoverished position and knew that he would never be able to raise the dowry needed for her marriage. She had to think about her own self and make her own arrangements for marriage. Zahra states, "My parents are not affluent. That is why I left home to marry the man of my choice. We fell in love first. I chose to get married to a Muslim man who was earning, skilled and healthy. The poverty of my parents encouraged me and supplied me with the conviction. I used my own powers. I depended on my strength of will to leave home and get married in secret without informing anyone" (Zahra Interview 2004). Her family kept up their ties with her and visits her occasionally. The marriage did not create any enmity.

Young women endeavor to avoid abuse and victimization that is often associated with arranged marriage, while elders consider themselves as victims of inter-caste and most egregious victims of inter-religious marriages. The free mixing of students in schools, colleges and the increase of college attendance is faulted as the cause for mixed unions. Mixing freely and secretly indulging in relationships is the root cause of friction between the elders and their children. A mother of young children fears for the future and informs me about her reasons. "Thanks to the free mixing young people have more courage today. They don't care for anybody; have no respect for elders or shame. They are quite desperate as a result of parental indulgence. Parents are catering to all unreasonable demands of their children, and thanks to overindulgence the lives of these kids are being spoilt. Their parents are accepting all the wrongdoings quietly; they don't dare to rebuke them lest they try something bad, like suicide" (Piyush Interview 2006). Middle-class families increasingly lavish luxuries on their children and expose them to a society where the children expect their families to fulfill their dreams. Parents point to the increasing moral degradation among young Bengalis these days. Adults complain that young people today lack serious thoughts. They neither have nor share the same ideals embodied in their parents and show no interest in social and cultural activities. Piyush has lost hope for the future of the youth, pointing out to me that, "They don't have any 'culture.' You can see them sitting and gossiping; some will work on computers, some will just chat and others will watch vulgar films in video parlors. This is the daily routine of young people. They do not think of their future. They don't have any 'high ambition.' They spare no serious thought on their future" (ibid).

To digress from the above bleak picture, I would add that the mindset of the present generation differs from that of their parents. Piyush comments that most children are selfish and self-centered and blames their socialization for their mean demeanor. What she means by meanness is their disrespect for their parents and community or, in general, the elders. Younger generations are presently pushing the limits of their freedom, not dissimilar from their parents who married against their cultural tradition. What I found out is an intriguing, conflicting theme that speaks to the current situation, as it emerged from many couples in mixed unions. There seems to be consensus as to what might be accepted behavior according to one's culturally constructed guideline. In case of a Hindu family (with an inter-caste marriage), the couples are clear about their position on the future marriage of their children and the boundaries of acceptability. Marrying a non-Hindu is unambiguously a taboo. They vehemently expressed their intolerance of such a union for the reason that the marriage is impure and affects the culturally delineated sacred Hindu spaces that would forbid the inclusion of a bride from another caste group. Introducing a bride, a woman from a different religion, poses problems to the specific family receiving the incoming new kin.

To illustrate this point, an example is often given of a lower caste woman who fell in love with an upper caste man and got married against stern objections from the man's family, a celebrated well-known case in the town. Even after 24 years they are barred from entering the paternal house and forbidden to worship the family deities. On another note we have examples of families who have not been able to allow daughters married to Muslim men or a son married to a Hindu woman enter their fathers' houses again, and here I refer to the case of Shweta Bibi and her husband Rahim as well as Rupa, whose interviews I have addressed earlier. Rupa, referencing to her past experience and the pain she endured, would not force her daughters to get married. She would consider allowing them to remain unmarried, which would be unprecedented. She says, "Why should I 'interfere' in their personal matters? I will never arrange their marriage by force. I am unwilling to take any step which is contrary to their liberty" (Rupa Interview 2005). However, as much as she is willing to cede ground on some aspects of marriage for her daughters, she is uncompromising on the issue of inter-religious marriage. She says that as long as her daughters choose a Hindu for a husband, she will not object to the difference in caste status. However, she added that she felt strongly about allowing her girls to choose a Muslim for a husband. She insisted that her objections to such unions rests on the foundation that Hindus and Muslims do not mix well, likening such a union to mixing oil and water, elements which do not mingle well. At the same time, I did not find any difference in the reaction of Rahim and Shweta when I broached the subject of their daughter selecting a non Muslim; although they chose to cross the religious line they will be against it when it comes to their daughter.

Meanwhile, I found many young women in particular giving their future serious thought. Some went as far as planning their own marriages because they strongly believe it is their responsibility to do so. The changes and complexity of the present generation's mindset are apparent. Many think of themselves first and society or family second. In this sense, they may be viewed by others as selfish and self-centered, but their own view is that they are forced into these situations because of their social condition. As a result, their behavior and actions are often seen to be mean and hurtful.

But the experiences of women in this society, adjusting to expectations at their in-laws' house, do not necessarily mean that their daughters will undergo similar experiences. The young generation is having to grapple with the choice to marry against their family. For this generation, the idea of adjustment to the will of strangers (one's in-laws) is difficult to embrace. A young woman who is used to a nurturing environment, and was allowed relative freedom in her upbringing, would find herself having to change her ways and beliefs, and, as Sonali observes, it would be difficult to enforce. "We'll see, ask her to adjust as much as possible—in case of real torture we'll take action, resort to legal steps. We'll bring her home. We can't abandon her. She is educated. She will try for a job. Then we'll decide according to the situation. I will never be able to keep her in her marital home forcibly" (Sonali Interview 2005). Precisely because of the unforeseen situation of violence and less of amicable living situations, the younger generation begins to rethink the values of arranged marriages.

Returning to the idea of a free act or to use the argument that it is one's right to decide whom to marry, these unending discussions of having to accept the distressing finality of one's daughters' free act does not sit well with many families in the town today. Adults, or in this case parents, declare that they alone know what is good for their daughters and try to make the best possible arrangements for their marriages. On the other hand, parents who themselves broke with tradition to marry a partner of their own choice have the strongest objection to their children emulating them and marrying their chosen grooms. According to these parents, hindsight has provided them with clarity of vision for them to regret that they did not listen to their parent's cautionary advice against mixed marriages. In effect, these parents' are just reliving the tradition of protecting their children against what they deem to be doomed unions. Since some parents disallow their daughters to choose their partner for marriage, they are apprehensive about their children's safety. No one can guarantee the well-being of one's daughter as there are many unknowns awaiting the new bride. Parents constantly worry if the choice they made for their daughter's marriage was the best. Did they choose for their daughter a decent man, an alcoholic, a gambler, or a man of loose morals? Parents always try to marry their daughter to an eligible groom. But they are always scared in case as parents they failed to find her a good husband. One mother, who is adamant that her daughter will have an arranged marriage, illustrates in the following quote this point of view: "There is no accounting for the number of women whose lives have been spoilt as a result of such marriages. That is why we are always apprehensive. This is what we are scared of. We will always hope for a decent marital home, a good husband who will make her happy. If she is happy in her marital home, the parents are at peace too" (Urmila Interview 2004).

Sonali, another concerned mother of a teenager, adds that amongst her major concerns and fears are the unforeseen negative qualities of an individual's character. Parents arrange their daughter's marriage to the best of their ability. "After that, a married woman's happiness and sorrow depend upon her fate. If she is lucky, she will have a happy, peaceful life, and if not, a veil of sorrow will envelop her. Parents cannot change their daughter's fate. She will enjoy or suffer the amount of joy or sorrow she is destined to have; not more, not less. As Hindus, we really believe in fate. If God is pleased, she will enjoy a happy married life" (Sonali Interview 2005). On the other hand, if a married daughter is unhappy in her martial condition, returning to her father's household is frowned upon.

Sonali, who accommodates ideas of "proper" behavior and following tradition adds, ". . . after marriage, a bride comes under the husband's control. She will have to follow his wishes. After marriage, a woman will have to take her husband's family name and *gotra* (Hindu scriptural family of sages). So she no longer belongs to her parents. After she is married, we cannot bring her home whenever we want. Her in-laws may not allow us to bring her even if we go there to get her. It falls under their right. This is why it is said that women are others' property, kept as collateral by parents. We bring her up, feed and clothe her, educate her and give her to someone else" (ibid).

A mother agrees that her children can at times make the correct choice, and refuse a husband chosen for them. The recognition of a child's right is acknowledged, but they place strong objections to the types of marriages that these young children might fall prey to and thus instigate chaos not just for her future but also to the families concerned. A lower caste woman who married an upper caste man said the marriage caused his family anguish, resulting in more than ten years of silence between the generations. She adds, "I will have strong objection if my daughter wants to have an inter-religious marriage. I am a Hindu. I don't even have any objection to an inter-caste marriage. I have immense respect for my own religion. I will never commit any anti religious act or allow my daughter to do it. It is mandatory for the man of her choice to be a Hindu. I will not accept it if he belongs to another religion. I am a Hindu kayastha, so my daughter has to marry a Hindu. She was born a Hindu and will die as one" (Piyush Interview 2006). This woman, who defied the wishes of her community and caused problems to her husband's family, will not allow her daughter the right to choose her partner if he happens to be a non Hindu. She will accept inter-caste marriage if she has to, but her family will never respect nor entertain someone from a different religion. Given the differences in Hindu cultural and dietary customs from other religious groups, Piyush finds it difficult to accept inter-religious marriages. In spite of the caste differences between her and her husband, she managed to adjust and made sure that their wedding followed Hindu rites. These were decisions they both agreed upon. She says, "I belong to the scheduled caste and my husband is a kayastha. My husband proposed to me. I also thought about it. Then I decided that he was good, able, earning well and of good character, so I would have a happy married life. Then we got married. This was how I thought before my marriage. But if I found out after my marriage that he was not as good as I had thought, that he was cruel and bad tempered, and that it was impossible to live with him, I would have divorced him" (ibid). Given that she had already crossed one barrier to marry her husband, she would not endure a bad marriage. Her own conscience would not allow her to stay in a marriage ridden with problems. For Piyush, divorce is an alternative, regardless of whether the marriage is acceptable or has crossed the caste and religious boundaries.

Questions surrounding independence of choice and the right to choose are mired in multiple layers of misunderstandings. Those affected use their own explanations according to their personal experiences and specific circumstances. A dissimilarity that I gathered from these stories is the fact that there are two types of marriages—arranged; and those that fall under the rubric of "love marriage," many of which are either inter-caste or inter-religious unions. Unmarried young girls do enjoy a semblance of freedom growing up in their paternal house; a free life lived with no worries or concerns. Young girls with no worries living amongst family members within familiar communities will experience major transformation if they disregard their tradition or rules of family code and conduct. Arranging their own marriage or going beyond the boundaries of family, caste or religion, the lack or refusal of acceptability will cause them grief and sorrow. The tranquil life they experienced in their father's house is unbalanced because they acted on their own free will, made a decision which disturbed the ties that bound them to family. The problem was simply put by Piyush: "I'll tell you a major defect of 'love marriages.' In case of a love marriage, the family never suffers. I've noticed in all love marriages I have seen that the family doesn't interfere. If it turns out well, then good, but in case the marriage doesn't succeed, people in the family say—'you've married by choice, now you solve it on your own, don't involve us.' They don't accept any responsibility or accord any help. But in case of 'negotiated' marriages, the parents have a lot of responsibility toward their daughters which they cannot ignore" (ibid). For many of the women who married on their own, they realize that though they made their choices against their parents' recommendations, they do not attain the same freedom after marriage. They are faced with newer concerns; the newer problems involve setting up a new life and confronting the challenges of a married life devoid of the familial environment and having to create new traditions nonetheless. Arranged marriages pose different impediments for a newly married woman. Immediately she gets married, her in-laws will inform her of cultural and kinship based restrictions. Her new life will not reflect a comparable lifestyle exercised in her father's house. She is limited in many ways, having to learn new ways of living and behaving. Couples often think that because one's family did not arrange their marriage, that it will bear different results. But soon that ideal or reasoning is quickly corrected by the conduct of the receiving families and one's husband. Those unions encounter similar problems and restrictions; the relayed stories inform me that at times life is the same as that of an incoming daughter-in-law whose marriage was arranged. Married women come to terms with having to address the challenges of the life cycle rites, whether their marriage was arranged or otherwise. Rarely will a woman who married for love find herself enjoying her independent decision, devoid of input from those who raised and nurtured her. In fact, her life is not easy but rather difficult because she lacks the support to safeguard her life and decisions. She is in a situation where, having made a free choice to marry and select her partner, she ends up at the mercy of others, who at times may not have her best interest at heart. She enters a new married life, inhabits a space where she will have to battle the anger of her new in-laws (if she is allowed to live with them), or focus on how to gain knowledge of a new religion (in case of conversion) and their societal norms.

Piyush informed me that if her daughter was to marry outside of her own religion, ". . . she can never come to her parental home again nor will we have any connection with her. Her own brother can never accept a Muslim brother-in-law. The ultimate result will be that the doors of her parental home will be closed for her forever. She will never be able to enter this house. We can never 'adjust' with her marital family or relatives. That will create some embarrassment for her. Men control our society, so when a woman gets married, she has to follow the norms of her marital home—however independent she is. She has to go by their 'status' somewhat. Women can never enjoy independence whether in their parental or marital home" (ibid). It was different in her case, for she did go against her family and the norms of marriage for a schedule caste by her marriage to a Hindu upper caste man. She quickly found that she had to accommodate different traditions and norms, even though they were within the same religion. She acted on her own choice when she got married, but now finds herself not enjoying any freedom in her marital home. She is dependent on her husband for his guidance and advice on acceptable behavior in the home.

It is true that girls do have dreams of marriage and having a family, husband and children. Living on one's own is frowned upon.

This is exemplified by Piyush's words: "Unless they marry, how can women become women (fulfilled)? Our society will not accept children of unwedded mothers. In order to have a legitimate child a woman must marry. Very few women in India are single. Indian women have incredible tolerance. Because of that they ignore a thousand insults and humiliation, to carry on in their marital homes" (ibid). According to a few women, they do not stress the biological need for women to have children, but they are sure that men marry to satisfy their sexual need whereas women marry to become mothers.

In my discussions about adolescence and or future marriage, I found that many women expressed fears for their daughters, and these were genuine and real. Urmila refers to these kinds of fears by alluding to the Hindu scriptures which states that ". . . when a brother and sister become 'adults' they should not be allowed to stay in the same 'room' in the house. It is not right for even a father to stay in the same room with his adult daughter. So, boys and girls must stay in 'separate rooms' when they grow up. This is the rule" (Urmila Interview 2004). The more I am told horror stories of girls gone astray or those who defied their parents, I come to the same conclusion that raising a daughter is difficult. Household members of the community and the public share such reservations as well. Urmila referred to incidents of adolescence and sexual abuse in the town, stories I had not been privy to in my first experiences with fieldwork in this area. "It has been seen on many occasions that a father or a brother has been involved in illicit relationship with one's daughter or sister. We know of such incidents in Bishnupur. A father abused his daughter day after day. Adolescence is a frightening thing. Eighteen year olds do not understand what is good or bad for them. At this age they are unwilling to listen to reason. That is why parents have to act as friends, to guide their children. They must also keep a strict eye lest the children mix with bad company, because this is a dangerous age. At this age they are like soft clay. One can make idols as well as monkeys. You can give the wet pliant clay whatever shape you want as it is not fired and made strong" (ibid).

Parents' interpretation of their children's rebellious actions has less to do with their children enjoying freedom and more to do with adolescent immaturity. This, according to the parents, explains why some of the girls go astray and fall prey to illicit sexual attractions, as well as rogue decisions that include inter-caste and inter-religious marriages. Parents are frightened to see their children go through this "adolescent period," at which time boys and girls are perceived to be unable to accept sex education or even comprehend it in the context of how it is taught to them. No matter how much parents try to explain the changes that the adolescents are experiencing, during this period the adolescents themselves are resistant to the lessons. They also keep an eye on the adolescents least they fall into evil ways. Parents face problems claiming that their society is bombarded with illicit advertisements on TV and films which expose children to ideas challenging what the families attempt to teach them about life and its expectations. The West Bengal government has begun sex education in schools and has included sex education in the syllabus to make school children aware of sex life. Families think it is crucial that their children are taught about AIDS and other sexually transmitted diseases such as gonorrhea or syphilis. There is a consensus that sex education at school is crucial to increasing children's ability to make wise decisions about their sexuality. As one woman puts it, "If schoolchildren learn in advance about the frightful sexual diseases as a result of free mixing and 'indiscriminate sexual life,' their future sex life will be stable. After having sex education children are cautious and careful. Therefore, children should be taught from the primary stages" (Ratna Interview 2006).

Some parents are at a loss and fearful of their children's future because they dread the possibility of their daughter or son going astray. Sanjay says, "Kids are becoming more corrupt by watching distasteful things on TV and the Internet all the time; our children are losing their morals. The dirty sexy ads are forming adverse reactions in their young minds. And in time they start leading immoral lives. Suppose I am watching a good serial with my children and a sexy ad is on television it affects our children. Our children are becoming degraded as a result of such ads. They create sexual arousal, which they want to fulfill 'practically' whenever they get a chance. They are establishing physical relationships with each other before marriage" (Sanjay Interview 2006).

It is a fact that one sees many more girls out in the open, walking unaccompanied by adults, which for many is a new experience. The liberty to allow them to walk unaccompanied is beginning to generate concern for some of the parents. A father of unmarried girls articulated his concerns, confirming that his daughters move about town to school, college, or various coaching centers after school on their cycle. The times are different from those 30 to 35 years back. Then, he said, ". . . there wasn't such free mixing between boys and girls. Now thanks to going to schools, colleges and coaching together, there is unlimited association. I am almost 60 now. In our times, if we had to speak to an unmarried girl, we had to keep a careful lookout lest we were being 'followed.' It was considered a social crime to talk to unmarried young women without a particular reason" (A concerned father Interview 2006). He complained that the freedom granted to the girls is causing serious disruptions within families and yet, they cannot prevent their daughters from going to school or taking up tuition. There are parents who are keenly observant that generally student life happens to coincide with the adolescent period for all girls. This is the time when various physical and mental changes occur. Parents or guardians agree that during this time young impressionable girls fall in love with boys from a different caste. In turn, the girl would inform her father not to negotiate for her marriage since she has already chosen her husband. Ratna reiterates that these days girls do not wait for their parents' consent, but simply leave home and marry. Some do not even maintain contact with their parents after the marriage for the simple reason that the parents may not accept them. In cases of love marriages or inter-caste ones, children do not concern themselves with nor wait to hear the opinion of parents, except if the man they married leaves them. In such cases, girls will seek the support and shelter of their parents' home. A mother once told me that she is aware of the temptations a girl experiences. Times are different and difficult, yet there seems to be more freedom given to the girls. She frowns on the accessibility and free reign that girls seem to be given. She compares her own upbringing and states: "When we were eighteen, our parents used to keep strict vigilance on us, scolded us, beat us, all for our own good. Did it mean that they didn't love us? Of course they did. They would keep an eye on us to make our lives happy, lest we deviate from the right path. It was their responsibility to keep us in line. If you slip slightly at this age, your life will be ruined. Therefore, this age is dangerous. After crossing this age boys and girls know what is right and wrong in life. They realize what they should and shouldn't do. They are more self conscious, have more knowledge and maturity" (Ratna Interview 2006).

Freedom of mind and socialization of girls

I took part in many discussions about inter-religious unions of Hindu girls marrying Muslim men, and it was often the case that parents emphatically informed me that Hindu families would never accept them (inter-religious couple) and never allow them freedom to enter their (parents') house. But I also came to know girls who converted to Islam and lived happily in their husband's households. It is the elders' perceptions that the young girls are not aware of their actions. Their children's tendency to fall in love and marry Muslim men is faulted on the freedom that they accord these children. According to the elders, the education that young people receive is the cause of these mistakes, for if a girl is not educated she would not have a chance to meet boys from another community. Families attest that they are at fault, too, because they spoil their children by sending them to schools and colleges, offer them tuition and anything else they ask for. They did not except the children to exploit their freedom. As Sanjay says, "Bengali Hindu girls are marrying Muslim boys and living as Muslims. But any guardian or I will not accept it if my son marries a Muslim girl or allow her in the house. You won't find any Muslim daughter-in-law in a Bengali (Hindu) household. No Hindu parent will accept it" (Sanjay Interview 2006).

He agrees that Hindu girls are given too much independence, which is the cause of the problem. "I think these Hindu girls have too much freedom. At present, Hindu girls are getting much more love and care from parents and also a lot of money. That is why they are doing such nasty indiscretions. Being very liberal, Hindu Bengali girls don't care for casteism; they fall in love with Muslim boys and get married to them. But Muslim society is very orthodox. Muslim girls are forced to adhere to strict religious restrictions. They cannot mix freely with men, or go out as they wish. It is forbidden for unmarried girls to chat with unmarried boys. So they can't marry men from other castes" (ibid).

The interesting debate about the orthodoxy of Muslim families prohibiting Muslim girls marrying Hindu boys does have validity. It is true that Muslim girls are perceived as orthodox and at the same time illiterate, which should make it impossible for them to meet non Muslim men. The reality is that Muslim and Hindu girls attend the same colleges today. The only difference between the two communities is that the religious orthodoxy that the Muslim community has prescribed on their girls and women are comparatively more pronounced. They are expected to observe *purdah* outside the house and are not allowed freedom to move out of the house unaccompanied. A Hindu man said, "They have neither economic nor social freedom. In general, they do not dare to have inter-caste (inter-religious) marriages. They are usually not promiscuous" (Sanjay Interview 2006). Compared to the Muslims, he blames his own community in allowing the girls unlimited freedom to the point that the freedom granted is now corrupting the youth to the extent that they lack discipline and reason. Instead of placing the blame on the woman for having exercised her freedom and making her own decisions, I have come across new reproaches, one of them being that parents have given their children too many liberties that were misused.

Conclusion: Is there a consensus about the idea of freedom for women and what the concept means?

It is difficult to wrap up the discussion of what the meaning of freedom is, and what the concept signifies to the men and women that I spoke to. How far is it truly an act of freedom to self-select a groom and go against tradition, when they still resort to a new set of traditions emerging from their particular situations and circumstances? The temporality and interpretation of a free act—defying their own cultural upbringing and immersing themselves in a new, untested and unfamiliar environment is a sure indicator of the enormity of their transformation from their accustomed way of life. To make the decision to marry entails confronting challenges and difficulties, contrary to the relative ease experienced when their parents plan their marriage for them. Moving out of "an easy life" in their parents' home, where all life's decisions are made for them is difficult for young women, as they have to adjust to problems arising from marrying a stranger to the family, caste, or religion. Interviews and discussions with some of the couples have proven that they have come to understand the results of their free choices, some with regret, while some found a way to deal with their particular circumstances and continue with their marriages. I find myself surprised at the strong reactions exhibited by couples that have undertaken either inter-caste or inter-religious marriage. These are the families that would not allow their children the luxury to make a decision to marry outside of the family's caste membership or religious beliefs. It is the same couples that married outside of their religion who become the strongest advocates against inter-religious marriages. Tradition and what it entails becomes their new dharma, and they have a new resolve to preserve it, even though having once gone against it. For those who were successfully accommodated into a new life (and religion, for those who converted to the religion of their husband), they understand the trials they endured and would not want the experience to be passed on to their children. Knowing what it meant to defy tradition and be cast away from those who nurtured and socialized them, these parents do not want to subject their children to that same experience. The experience of pain, hatred, marginalization, subjection to alienation from family and loved ones was insurmountable for some parents. Why would they allow their children to go through it? To them, the accepted wisdom is to think and act for their children following a process they themselves refused to adhere to at the time of their marriage. Notwithstanding the lack of guarantee that their children's marriage, if allowed to happen under the pretext of freedom (their own decision to marry out of love), would turn out as badly as theirs did, these parents face a difficult decision today. How different is this scenario? Are the steps to break from family and traditions so arduous and hard to accept for parents who have once made a break, that they now force their children to rethink similar decisions?

Notes

1. The young Santhal girl is the younger sister of Mary whom I interviewed in 2004.

Violence and Torture:
The Search for the Ideal
Way of Life

"There is fear of society. We are bound by social norms. We are always scared lest people in society criticize us. I may not subscribe to it. But everyone else does. Since I live here permanently I have to abide by the rules." (Lakshmi Interview 2005)

"A woman without a husband is like sand without the river. No man to protect you and every evil wind will blow over your body. Listen to your mother." (Rau Badami 1996: 159)

Fear of violence and the future

Fearing violence and anticipating torture when one enters an unfamiliar space are of utmost concern to young girls. Discussing violence was easier with the younger generation compared with their parents. Although the idea of violence seemed to be on everyone's radar, unmarried girls were able to articulate it better than their married counterparts. They were aware that they would be the new recipients of brutality if they ended up with the wrong in-laws and a less protective husband. Wide media coverage of issues concerning domestic violence and victimization of women has exposed the uncertain environment in which some women live. Incidents of violent behavior as experienced by women featured on TV screens—documentaries, news features and, more recently, exposure of Bollywood films focusing on vicious offences against women (not to mention the increase of pornographic films even in semi urban areas)—are on the increase. The explicit degradation and uncertainty of the women's fate in these features remain etched in the minds of many young girls about to enter a new life, or are close to leaving the safety of their father's house to commence the life of a married woman. When asked about their future, unmarried girls openly articulate that gender-based violence can occur within arranged and/or love marriages. Today, the subject of violence is frequently discussed in the context of marriage. When young girls tell me about their conflict and disagreement with arranged marriage (their refusal to yield to tradition), they repeatedly refer to the potential of violence in these unions, and their inability to protect themselves. Parents of young girls who themselves have gone through arranged marriages understand that times are different, and that they might not have been subjected to the kind of violence that women are currently subjected to. In short, all types of marriages are subjected to the same criticism and condemnation; that there is no guarantee of a perfect marriage which will protect women from violence. Most married women indicate that they have either heard of or experienced some form of violent behavior in their in-laws' house. Some of these narratives are often reported in the media or shown on television, representing the occurrences of violent behavior towards married women. Daughters-in-law are often the victims in these stories, in which their cries are heard by many, yet the tradition of marriage continues to be perpetuated in the hope that the bride will experience an ideal marriage characterized by trust and optimism. How do we understand these fears vis-a-vis the choices young girls make regarding the unknown conduct of one's partner? Despite all of the public discussion of violent behavior within marriage, it appears that the idea of marriage has not been devalued. Unmarried girls continue to take up the challenge and make their untraditional, self-selected marriage choices.

Women endure humiliation and pain, especially because many are financially dependent on their husbands. These ordinary housewives are forced to bear their husband's torture without protesting to their own family or their in-laws. Married women say that they are helpless when it comes to voicing complaints about their circumstances. They lack the resources to present their case in court, and when they are able to go to court, their husbands find out about the cases, and they (the husbands) bribe the judges and police to stop the case against them. A victimized married woman who had faced an impasse with her situation said, ". . . with money and power, my husband (can) arrange to murder me. That apart, where would I get the money to pay the fees of a lawyer? I don't have money to maintain myself, nor to buy clothes, let alone medicines in the event of an illness. As we don't have economic freedom, women are humiliated and harassed, tortured physically and mentally at every step. There is no remedy" (Meenu Interview 2006).

But the idea of being single, unmarried, is equally a problem for women, as they live in a society that expects girls to marry as adults, no matter what the outcome. A woman told me that it was her understanding that perhaps five percent of all marriages have positive outcomes, where the couple enjoys good understanding with each other and their children. She said, "You may find 5 good families out of 100, but 95 are bad. There is no guarantee that love marriages will be happy. In most cases we see a lot of problems. Whether arranged or love marriages, one finds many problems" (Shanti Interview 2006). Many women remain trapped in their unbearable marriages and learn to tolerate and bear the pain inflicted upon them. For some, divorce is not an option, taking into account the lives and safety of their children. In case a married woman walks out of a marriage, her problems are insurmountable. One ponders over why a woman whose marriage is traditionally arranged, leaves her father's house to reside at her in-laws' place as their daughter-in-law and the mother of their grandchildren, in the knowledge that the chances of violence in that arrangement are extremely high. It is not clear who should bear the blame for these unlawful acts. Take the scenario that a Hindu woman is given in marriage by her father in accordance with the rites of marriage of the Hindu religion. In case the married Hindu woman leaves her husband's place and marriage, her husband and his family would not support the children. She would have to assume the responsibility of having to raise them on her own, which is a very difficult task given the woman's financial dependency. In such a situation, is bearing the pain her best option? In any case, are married women today ready to tolerate the abuse against them? Are they ready for some sort of activism that could be used to force an improvement to their lives? (See Jeffery and Basu 1998; Jeffery and Jeffery 1996 who have addressed some of these questions.)

An educated married woman once told me, "If we go against our husbands they will beat us and drive us out. We can't apply any force on them. We must cater to them, love them and stay with them. We can't judge their acts or protest. Unless ordinary housewives like us bow to our husbands, we won't have anywhere to go. Even if my husband goes on making mistakes, I can't protest. There is no law and order particularly in West Bengal. It used to be slightly better before the Communist Party Marxist (CPM) (the then ruling party) rule. Now it is awful" (Ratna Interview 2003). What is the fate of women who arranged their own marriages and severed ties with their own families? Whose law will now protect them? Where are their fathers and brothers who could have intervened and addressed their abuse and dealt with the abusers?

I met a woman whose husband took a second wife openly; he lives with the second wife and their children. The man is educated and has an excellent position that pays him well, but refuses to care for his first family. Legally, a married woman owns half of the marital joint property but this law did not provide meaning or protection to the first wife. She could continue to reside in the husband's house, but because of the unpleasant condition, it would be difficult for her to stay. Through the Women's Committee or "court," the government allows her the right of half of all joint shares. Yet, even if she wanted to sell her share, nobody would buy it because, as she explained, no one wants to buy "disputed land or property" and get into trouble. People with practical sense would not invest or spend money on disputed land. "With the help of law, I can get half of my husband's property. But the law will not come to see how I can enjoy my share. I can get all the 'legal documents,' but the 'court or administration' will not come to check it in person. The court will give me the deeds, but they won't come to verify if I am getting it. If I make too much noise, my husband will kill me at night and hang me" (ibid). A man once told me, "the life of a woman is like the saw of the conch shell craftsmen—it cuts both ways." He added that women are not considered as human beings in India.

In seeking to find alternative forms of marriage to arranged marriages, young girls do not always consider that their new found joy or their freedom in selecting their own partners could only be momentary. Fearing an encounter with violence, young women carefully manage to avoid experiences which might expose them to aberrant behavior by choosing their partner instead of agreeing to an arranged marriage. In a way, these brave women seek newer solutions to resolve older or unwanted problems. If a wife is tortured, I am told, whether she resides in her marital home or in a separate residence, she would have to accept the torture without a word of protest. Were she to inform her parents, they will immediately remind her that the marriage which is causing her problems was a result of her own choices and so she would have to bear with the circumstances. Being told to bear pain and torture is difficult, especially if the advice comes from one's parents. The situation gets worse when girls are unable to tolerate further harassment, and some end up killing themselves. The law today will blame the in-laws for domestic crimes and death of women. The mothers-in-law are arrested on charges of bride killing and torture.

There is a strong belief that women are naturally subservient to their husbands and they are bound to obey their husbands' "orders," whether right or wrong. It is worse in cases of women who are totally dependent on their husbands because they lack economic freedom. Women who lack financial self-reliance are bound to depend on their husbands, and thus may have inadequate freedom to act in their own defense when confronted with oppression. They are neither able to stand up for themselves, nor are they equipped with power to protest if the husband offends them. This scenario reflects the most common condition of married women within "mixed unions," including those within arranged marriages. While rejection of arranged marriages by young girls is done for fear of being exposed to unknown tribulations, it is now apparent that newly married girls who have made their own marriage decisions find themselves facing similar circumstances—vulnerable to the exposure of violence in their own non-traditional arranged marriage. It is a fact that even in love marriages women face the possibility of torture. Parents will rebuke their son for having brought in a wife without a dowry, because most love marriages do not bring in any form of dowry. The remark one hears often is that the girl has married their son for love, thus her parents did not have to pay any dowry or gifts to the groom's side. Piyush reiterates how parents bemoan the union, saying "'Our son has just married the girl empty handed, depriving us of a lot. We could have got a lot of money, gifts and gold ornaments had we arranged a marriage for him. So the woman is a scheming, clever person who hasn't brought us anything. We have incurred much loss.' Then she is tortured mentally, in some cases physically as well and there are constant problems because of non-payment of dowry" (Piyush Interview 2006).

No matter which of the two communities I held interviews with, couples in mixed union always brought forth the question of greed, and that greed was often connected to the increase of violence against women. One hears stories of couples who, though they had gone through arranged marriage, were found to have problems when the husband, propelled by greed, tortured his spouse physically and/or mentally, demanding that his wife secure additional money from her parents or face the consequence of torture. Torturing women has become a daily news item in national and local papers. In a number of the reported cases, the married woman, unable to bear the torment, eventually resorts to suicide. To dissuade young girls from marrying outside their religion or caste, parents point out the difficulties that do and can occur within love marriages as well. These include the fact that parents will not interfere in their daughter's troubled marriage; they cannot come to her aid nor assist to sort out her misunderstandings or differences with her husband.

This is not an exaggeration; it is a well-known fact that women face torture even in love marriages. Confirming to the multiple discussions I held, many couples attested to the occurrence of violence within love marriages. It is true that in "negotiated marriages" the man and woman are completely "unknown" to each other as they are initially strangers. The absence of adequate information and transparency about the family one marries into leaves the incoming daughter-in-law vulnerable. Many young girls are weary of arranged marriages because of the minimal interaction between the families and the couple before marriage. However, it seems that their desire to escape such marriages does not necessarily reduce their vulnerability to violence and torture. When a boy marries a girl from a different caste and/or religion, he brings her home to his family hoping that they would wholly accept her. Accepting a total "stranger" with whom one had no initial contact is not easy for many families. In case the bride is not accepted or welcomed wholeheartedly, she certainly starts her married life in a vulnerable position. She is constantly reminded of the chaos and humiliation that her arrival caused to the community, to their religious groups, their caste and the immediate household. At the outset, her husband does protect her and often bears all the abuse alongside his wife because he too is implicated and accused of what has transpired. However, men, unlike their wives, have options. Married women move out of their fathers' house to that of their husbands, a journey that is undertaken only once in their lifetime. Having executed their freedom to marry against their parental wishes, they are now confronted with the consequences of their actions, most of which take the form of mental and physical abuse. While women are expected to learn to endure pain and hardship, men seek alternatives. Men are aware that their wives are vulnerable as they are financially dependent on them. Some men take advantage of the situation and act irresponsibly. A young man tells me that men in higher positions and professions tend to renege on their family duties and responsibilities. "However educated or pretty a woman is, if she doesn't have a job or is earning an income, such housewives have no right to protest or speak against their husbands. If her husband marries thrice, she can't protest. She is a housewife, totally dependent on her husband. She can see only if he is taking care of all her needs. That is why, in spite of all the torture (physical and mental) and cruelty, she will have to bear it silently all her life. These ordinary housewives have no other shelter because they don't have any income" (Sanjay Interview 2006). I was not surprised to hear this comment; in fact I had heard stories of men who openly take two wives. On the other hand, there are cases of women in arranged marriages seeking respite in the law, though it is not a route commonly taken. Married women living in a contentious marriage situation find it very difficult to speak up or find a way to rectify their situation.

Despite women's families paying the entire demanded dowry, men extract additional sums, especially if there is a chance that more can be forced out of the woman's family. Presently, in arranged marriages where dowry is expected, the amount of the dowry has reached such proportions that it is very difficult to get girls from ordinary middle class families married off. Many families are unable to secure the demanded amount of dowry, leaving their daughters past the marriageable age. "Spinsters spend their lives working as unpaid maids in their brothers' families. They do not have many problems while their parents are alive, but after their deaths they bring up their brothers' children and do servile work, live without any dignity and honor. As a consequence of the patriarchal society and given importance to marriage, along with the ever-increasing dowry amounts and higher number of unmarried women, all of these accumulated problems cause social problems as well. The number of rapes is higher, and as dowry demands remain unfulfilled, torture and murder of wives is increasing. The root cause of torture of women is this horrible dowry system" (ibid).

There are parents who have religiously followed all of their tradition and caste rules but are still not at peace after the marriage of their daughter. At times, within a month's stay at her marital house, a married woman discovers that her father- and mother-in-law show signs of greed and begin to pressure their daughter-in-law with newer demands, for example ". . . the furniture and gifts you have brought from your parents are of very inferior quality. Your parents haven't given you the amount of gold jewelry we had asked for. You must get more money from them" (ibid). The nature of violence a woman experiences differs depending on who she is and what type of marriage she entered into. In order to avoid arranged marriages, with the expectation that they would be exempt from paying dowry, women proceed to marry outside the boundaries of tradition and religion. The choice and the responsibility are theirs, and although the decision was made as a couple, the woman suffers more than her husband. Her narrative is different and it is a mix of joy and pain. Hers is a story with no solution, most of the times she remains in the household and learns to speak less of her predicament. Absent in her social surroundings are her father or brothers, men who under ordinary circumstances would vow to uphold and protect their daughter or sister, respectively.

Usually any union which is not within one's caste or religious boundaries will cause unwarranted number of problems for the couple as well as the communities in question. Those who accept an incoming bride from a different caste or religion face the consequences of both abuse and harsh treatment from caste and religious groups. On the other hand, families who lost a daughter through such a marriage are exposed to abuse because they are seen to be unable to contain or marry their daughter in accordance with their tradition. Family members are often blamed as bad parents for failing to advice their daughter who strayed. In the case of a high caste woman marrying a lower caste man, the groom's community is apprehensive concerning the ensuing chaos the marriage would cause. Bringing an upper caste woman into a lower caste community obviously disrupts the kinship based rules and prompts the lower caste in-laws to assert a different mode of behavior, contrary to what they are socialized to observe towards people of a higher caste. For a lower caste family accepting an upper caste daughter-in-law who has been incorporated into their own *gotra*, the dilemma is how they should relate to her hierarchically. Kinship rules dictate that the incoming wife acts deferentially to her in-laws, but when she is of a higher caste, how then will that issue be resolved? The caste issue causes them social problems and the ensuing confusion leaves them at a loss initially. Normally, the wife receivers do not come across these readjustment problems and do not have to rethink their kinship rules of conduct. Lower caste families are apprehensive and, at times, uncertain of future relations with upper caste families by whom they might be employed. This issue was brought to my attention many times during the research, in particular when the bride came from a much higher caste. The joy of receiving a bride eventually causes tremendous constraints and pain to the accepting in-laws' families.

Tolerance for abusive relations: Are there alternatives for women today? Narratives of victims

Courageous women, who sought to solve their own life's problems by avoiding arranged marriages and denying the grooms' families the right to demand dowry, ended up learning hard lessons. Some of these strong willed women regretted the choices they made and quickly made sure that their own children would not be permitted such liberties. Parents who had made mixed marriages tended to be strict about the future of their own children; these children will most likely have a tough time marrying outside their religion or caste. Having gone through rough times and hardships, adjusting to anger and humiliation themselves, these families expressed fear for their children's future.

Piyush told me that, as far he was concerned or aware, regardless of the type of marriage that a woman underwent, the eventuality of suffering was inescapable. Marriage executed with a gift of dowry does not guarantee that the bride will be safe in the union. If the girl's parents are unable to fulfill the groom's demands, the girl will experience various forms of torture. Her parents foresee this kind of scenario occurring and try to mitigate the likelihood of it by borrowing money or selling off land or other property to meet the dowry demands. Oftentimes they have no alternative. Impelled by excessive greed, the boys' parents pressurize the girls' parents and extract money from them. In case no money is forthcoming, the girl is made to suffer, and is tortured both physically and mentally. This is a common method of extracting additional dowry beyond the stipulated original amount agreed upon, that is often paid before the marriage is formalized.

It is true that not all women are tortured in their matrimonial homes. It is also true that a girl will be at peace if a lot of dowry is paid to the groom's side. Women are known to have suffered pain and abuse; all of this criminal behavior is caused by greed and demand for more dowry and gifts or additional gold jewelry by the groom's family. At times, this situation pushes women unable to bear the insult, torture and abuse, to their death—either through suicide or murder committed by a member of the groom's family. On a daily basis, there are different stories of torture, murder and rape of women shown on TV, reported in national or local papers, or told through word of mouth. This exposure of torture is unlike the scenario 30 years ago, when the townspeople were not generally aware of gender-related abuses and such narratives never came up in my discussions with them about their daughters or their marriages. Despite the Government of India anti dowry law, we find that the amount of money extracted for "expected" dowry has increased disproportionately against the cost of living. Lakshmi, a respondent, says a bit more about her own experience with torture; even after giving everything that the groom's side demanded the newly married woman was still tortured (Lakshmi Interview 2005). Some of the in-laws have become so greedy and shameless that they keep asking their daughter-in-law to bring more "wealth." If she fails to heed to their requests, she is then tortured. Unable to bear the inhuman torture she either leaves and goes home, or commits suicide. Either way, the in-laws proceed to arrange another marriage for their son, in which they will ask for more dowry.

Jaya is an example of an abused woman who tolerates her tortured life. She understands her legal rights as stipulated within the law, but chooses not to seek legal redress to her problems. Her account of abuse is immense; she points out that the ultimate blame is her own society which is dominated by men, offering women no rights, and especially for those women who do not earn an income independently. She said, "If an 'unemployed' woman acts or speaks against him (husband), he will immediately ask her to leave him" (Jaya Interview 2006). The fears expressed by Jaya are real, and exemplify the situation for many women who feel trapped in a difficult situation and regret their choice of marriages. Although Jaya tried to befriend her in-laws, they shunned her and would not accept her as an incoming wife. She has not maintained any ties with her in-laws, who have not behaved well towards her and continue not to include her in any of their life cycle rites or annual Hindu festivities. Though she lives close to their house, there is no visiting with them. "I am a Christian by religion. The Milkman caste of my husband don't approve of me. They don't like me visiting their area. My husband's brothers and sisters-in-law do come here. I am hurt that he has built our house in his old neighborhood instead of somewhere else and I am upset that I have to live in great hardship in a dilapidated earthen house. Yet if I speak out (against this condition), it will be crossing the limits, so I keep quiet" (ibid).

A woman in her eighties, from a well-known family in Bishnupur town, slowly recounts her life's experience. At the age of twelve she was given away in marriage to a man from an established rural landowning family. She recalls her encounter with extremely harsh treatment from her in-laws. Harassment and constant taunting from her in-laws led to mental abuse of the young bride, who could not bear the pain. At eighty years of age and looking back at her life back then, the old woman could not believe what she had endured. She said that given the intolerable situation she found herself in, her only option was the one she took. "I got so much ill and inhuman treatment, torture, and impolite behaviour from them that I could not express in words. I never harbored such type of conception in my mind. I cannot imagine that aforementioned incident transpired in a reputable, learned family. They were so bad, that not only did they daily beat me but they caused the loss of one of my fingers" (Bina Interview 2005). Courageously, one day, she walked out of her in-laws' house and returned to her paternal home. Regardless of being the only daughter from a reputable musician family, with a long ancestral history and excellent credentials, she was nevertheless treated brutally by her in-laws. Clearly the family's placement, or rank in society, did not prevent the violence she suffered.

Against her will and at an early age, Bina was given away in marriage. Her in-laws did not control themselves, but treated her badly and constantly beat her. "They tortured me physically and mentally. The character of my husband was very bad. He was lascivious, a drunkard. All I received was inhuman behavior from my father-in-law's family" (ibid). In his drunkard state, her husband would beat her incessantly with a stick, usually for no apparent reason. Her own father, having come to know of her treatment, had no misgivings in accepting his married daughter back home, where she spent the rest of her life attending to him and doing the household chores.[1] It is indeed remarkable that her parents, given the times and the conservative nature of their society, did not opt to send her back to her in-laws' house. The victimized young bride became known for her musical talents and was appreciated by visitors from Germany, Japan, USA, and from around India. She was pleased with her fame and accomplishments, but equally proud of how accomplished she was in taking care of household duties and cooking. She dabbled in painting as well, when she had the time.

Bina did not see herself as a feminist, nor did she raise this point with me during her interview. Her actions defied her in-laws who had accepted a new bride, and began to abuse her. Having taken a bold decision, one that was totally counter to the expectation of tradition, she asserts, eighty years later, that she had no regrets for her decision to leave her in-laws' house. People in the town recall Bina's story, mainly because of the great consternation that her actions provoked, but also because many people were not pleased with her. Most married women at that time would have resigned themselves to the life their married journeys took them upon, to endure the violence quietly. Compare Bina's story with that of Jaya's, the Christian woman who was married twice, and continues to lament her sorry married life, though she is not ready to publicly embarrass her husband by leaving.

Violence against women in Bengal knows neither religion, caste nor class. Men and women have recounted cases they know in which a bride was tortured or killed. Piyush says, "Women are tortured, secretly murdered for dowry money. Nearly two or three years back such an incident took place in Station Road in Bishnupur. Four years ago in Sankharibazar (a neighborhood in Bishnupur) a newly married woman's marital family killed her. As her father was unable to provide the dowry money, she was beaten by her in-laws and her husband. They placed a lot of pressure on her. Fearing the outcome of the inhuman torture, she went to her father to get the money. Her father was too poor to give it. She came back empty handed. When the in-laws came to know that she didn't bring any money, they burnt her late at night. The news spread in her neighborhood and the police came and took her dead body away. Her parents were informed. The police took statements, investigated and arrested her in-laws and her husband. The police started a case against them and they are still in prison" (Piyush Interview 2006).

In another case Urmila, a learned lower caste woman who married above her caste, raised her two daughters, pushing them to be academic achievers and seek employment before their marriage. Of course, like many mothers, she fears for their future. She hears and knows about some girls who ended their lives violently. In one of our meetings she recounted the story of a young married woman who was burnt by her in-laws in her house. "The couple was not compatible. They had constant friction. She was sleeping in a room in the house in the afternoon. They poured kerosene on her as she slept and shut all the doors and windows and burnt her alive. All of us went to see this. The police came later, and arrested everyone. Even now the husband of the victimized housewife is serving a sentence. The neighbors had planned to lynch the family after watching the horrible incident, but the police came in and persuaded the neighbors to cooperate with them in this brutal incident in which the government agencies were requested to impose the harshest punishment on the murderers" (Urmila Interview 2004). But not all violence is physical in nature. Violence comes in various forms and in many shades. I am informed that an employed and independent married woman is in a better position in her in-laws' house because she provides them with a monthly income. In another case, a school teacher who had an inter-caste marriage, earned a salary of about Rs. 6000, but she had no independence. Whenever she "draws her salary," immediately her husband would deposit the money in his account. She was given no right to spend her own hard-earned money. If she required money and asked her husband, he would deny her request and not even allow her any pocket money. Although her parents were not well off, her husband would not allow her to help her parents and the wife gave in to her husband's demands. A similar covert torture is refusing to allow one's daughter or son to live (next to their parents) in localities in which they grew up. The couples are marginalized because of their unapproved marriage. Punishing a couple for their acts in this manner adds to their pain. Their parents reject them and refuse them permission to reside or set up residency in the neighborhood where they grew up. Understanding the meaning of marginality and its consequences goes beyond the verbal abuse they are exposed to with regards to their decision to marry against parental expectations. Couples who have entered into an inter-caste or inter-religious marriage seek alternative housing areas to reside. The town is growing, spreading on the outskirts, where newer communities grow on the margins of the town. They are separated from older *paras* (neighborhoods) representing older families and today still recognized by their old names. Couples of mixed unions confront the difficulty of taking up residency in their ancestral house as many parents, though not all, and the members of the larger religious communities object to housing couples that have entered mixed unions, despite the conversion to the "right" religion. For an incoming bride to a Muslim household, conversion to Islam is not enough for a family to forgive the couple. For example, Rahim who secretly married a brahman girl now regrets his actions for he has been forced to be away from his mother and other relatives. In hindsight, he clearly sees what his actions meant. He states, "My mother was upset. She had brought me up and I married without letting her know. All mothers have dreams for their son's marriage; that they would select a bride, have a gorgeous wedding, have fun. She was sad and for that she didn't allow me entry into her house" (Rahim Interview 2006). For him, this form of punishment is hard to accept. He is happy in his marriage, in which he has two children. However, he needs more than that—his mother's love—but it seems that this affection has been denied to him.

When young men and women are asked if there are any regrets at having gone against the family's wishes and married across religious lines, few would answer in the negative, offering no "self-introspection" regarding their marriage. Despite the fact that a few of these couples are deprived of ancestral property and familial ties, they bear no regrets regarding what they have done. Usually, they give their situation serious thought only on occasions when they experience extreme hardship, like a case of caring for a sick child with no assistance from family members. It is at times like these that I would hear a couple express·regrets and vow to protect their own children against similar marriages in the future. "I will try to advise and educate my daughters from their childhood so that they are not misdirected, to be aware of their own interest and not to be cheated. I will discuss with them what is right and wrong, good and bad, and steer them on the right path. If they are educated and socialized early, they will listen to me. But if I indulge them now or allow them to have their way in everything then they will be spoiled. I have to keep them under control and not loosen the reins. If children follow their parents' good advice, the number of these inter-caste marriages can come down. They will be a little scared to transgress their parents' advice" (Meera Interview 2004). Obviously, her remarks touch upon her negative experiences resulting from her own mixed union, in which she found herself cut off from her previous community, caste and family as well as her husband's Muslim community, whose religion she had adopted after marriage.

Hearing different narratives attesting to the anguish women experience, I asked them why, these same women, now as mothers, would replicate the ideals they refused to follow. Why would they insist that their daughters marry in accordance with the family's wishes (taking up the newly imbibed tradition of their husband)? Although these mothers have earned their "freedom" in making their own choices for a marriage partner, when the focus and attention is their children's future, their tendency is to deny them their freedom to choose their partners in marriage. I was told over and over again that women have no independence, and from their birth most girls are insulted, humiliated and tortured. It is true that before marriage most girls enjoy parental love and care, but after marriage almost all encounter forms of torture in their matrimonial homes. My question then was—since many of the middle-class women underwent torture and humiliation in marriage, or even murder in some cases, why was marriage a necessity? Why do their parents arrange their marriage? What is the harm if they remain single? I queried a married woman who happened to be happily married and her answer only added to my astonishment, "For us Hindu women, we have no other alternative. All parents get their daughters married after ascertaining a good family and decent groom. No parent wants his or her daughter to stay unmarried all her life. There will be public criticism if a girl is not married off at an appropriate age. Then, most Indian women are not highly educated; without an independent income or a decent job who will look after them after their own (the parents') death? That is why they are eager to arrange their marriage and provide them with social security" (Lakshmi Interview 2005).

The occurrences of bride burning or torture were not very common in Bengal, though that is changing now. It is commonplace to see reports of murder, torture and suicide of housewives everyday in the news. Lakshmi goes on to explain, "These incidents are prompted by greed and the horrible dowry system. The girl is brought home with a fat dowry. After some time everybody in the family, her husband included, starts putting pressure on her to get more money from her home. If she is not able to bring money, she is tortured or even killed, and in some cases, she kills herself. After her death the husband gets married again, taking more dowry from someone else. So, one thing is clear: 'Dowry system' is at the root of all these crimes in society" (ibid). Are mothers hoping that they make a sound choice for their daughter in giving her in marriage? Are they shunning away from future responsibilities for their unmarried daughters? When faced with uncertainties for their unmarried daughters, is marrying them off to a strange household the best way to safeguard their social security in life, knowing full well that young girls object to the traditional approach to arranged marriages?

Adjusting to marriage, or to the new household, with new relatives and way of life is not easy for a new bride. To comprehend or come to terms with an entirely new situation is daunting. Parents of marriageable girls do worry about their daughter's happiness. Some newly married women adjust easily, enduring all odds, and there are cases of happy unions where everything turns out well. Newly married women are apprehensive of entering a household with many unmarried girls. For some of the married women, it is expected that they work for both the men and women in their new household. After their initial introduction into the house, the mother-in-law is expected to run the daily household chores with the help of a daughter-in-law, but they take advantage of the daughter-in-law and make her do all the chores. Recently, Piyush retold a story of his seven unmarried sisters who wanted their only brother to bring a bride into the house to serve them. He said, "My sisters had only one idea—'we would get our only brother married to a girl who will always be under our control and will be an unpaid maid servant, working tirelessly without complaint.' This was what my sisters wanted. That, my wife, should obey all their commands; she mustn't be very intelligent or sharp but slightly dumb. It would be very convenient. All my sisters had such a mentality" (Piyush Interview 2006).

Normally all married women wish to die before their husbands, fearing to be widowed. A woman who is in an abusive relationship welcomes widowhood. If she is miserable in her married life, she is certain that her life will not improve after her husband's death. I came across a woman who welcomes the stigma of widowhood willingly, and has vowed to bear the dishonor. Despite hearing all of the accounts of mistreatment and neglect, she has continued to refuse the offer of sanctuary from her family. She entered into her second marriage, arranged by her father, accepting a proposal from the man who promised to protect and safeguard her daughter from her first marriage. "I feel that I had made a mistake in marrying this man. He has spoilt my entire life. I tell him—you needn't have married me to help us in this way. He never fulfilled his duties. He doesn't have a good heart" (Jaya Interview 2006). She would not contemplate publicly denouncing her husband, nor lodge a complaint with the police despite the physical abuse she encountered. In her estimation (and correctly so) a public denouncement of her husband's doings would impair the "house," the family's name, and damage the honor of the lineage. In fact, tradition has not changed much and little progress has been made concerning the question of allowing women gender-based alternatives. Women's bodies do not belong to them, they are attached to lineality, caste, and kinship principles; they underlie the pure and the sacred attribute of the male line. In short, we find that what the female body represents ". . . was still pure and unmarked, loyal to the rule of the *shastras*" (Sarkar 2001: 43). Of course, the new generation of women view things differently and are cognizant of their rights and different ways to access the law. If they encounter torture, women immediately complain at the police station and the police do address their cases. Whereas in the past married women would have tolerated being tortured without a word, today some of the abused married women go so far as to cause the imprisonment of their in-laws as well as their husbands. It is true, as many inform me, that women are no longer powerless. They have the power to protest, although not many take that path for a variety of reasons. Fear to act on their own behalf overcomes them and thus they fall prey to the violence and torture. Denis Kandiyoti argues that generally women ". . . may be controlled in different ways in the interests of demarcating and preserving the identities of national/ethnic collectivities" (Kandiyoti 1991a: 382). Part of the patriarchal control plays out in the tacit silence in which women choose to remain instead of seeking legal redress to their problems. Women, being the preservers of culture and tradition, maintain the culturally prescribed gender-based code of conduct. "The identification of women as privileged bearers of corporate identities and boundary markers of their communities has had a deleterious effect on their emergence as full-fledged citizens of modern nation-states" (ibid: 388). Following the cultural dictates, women lack equal participation in the wider workings of society, and at times they cannot speak for themselves.

Yet, one does find husbands who fear displeasing their wives. If a particular habit, such as smoking or drinking, bothers a married woman, her husband would consider not engaging in the habit in front of her, but might do so outside the house because of her objections. One of these husbands once told me that his wife was against his drinking habits, which he had developed before marriage. He gave up those habits. "I must perform all my duties to the 'family'; look after her well-being. I must keep a vigilant eye on my two daughters, take care that they get good education, are self-reliant and have a happy future" (Raj, Lakshmi's husband, Interview 2005). He tries to include his wife in some of his outings, he socializes with his wife outside the house when they attend life cycle ceremonies, or occasionally go to eat out in the local hotels (not a custom one often sees among many married couples). This husband makes sure to take his wife out to visit friends and relatives, but he will not allow his wife to continue taking music lessons, a passion she had to forgo after their marriage. Being considerate to his wife will not signify allowing her to dishonor the family's tradition. Lakshmi claims, for the sake of tranquility, she did not pursue her music lessons. She gave up the idea of furthering her passion for studying music, even though she grew up with an appreciation for music in her father's family. She adds, "What will others say if his wife goes to learn music and sing in different functions? I have a lot of opportunities to learn high standards of music here. Ramasaran Music College is very close to my house. In spite of so many opportunities, I haven't been able to pursue music practice. The only reason is my husband's objection. I have had to stop (my music ambition) with a lot of pain and regret because of my marital family and my husband. There are families who don't approve of their women (daughters-in-law) going out to learn music. That is why my husband didn't want me to go out to learn and so he prevented me from doing so" (Lakshmi Interview 2005). Once again, I heard the same assertion that women try hard to avoid unpleasantness, and prevent relationships from deteriorating. Women give up their wishes and aspirations, stopping music or dance after their marriage, if a family disapproves of those hobbies. The women end up denying themselves, and stop pursuing their desires and passions.

When we think of the violence young couples experience when they revoke their own tradition of religious boundaries, we forget that their families are equally involved in those decisions and outcomes, despite the fact that some of the family members had no knowledge of the marriages. The members of the larger family confront the parents in question under whose watch unapproved unions were allowed to occur. In the end, all of the couple's kin become entangled in the consequences of unapproved marriages. The consequences of those acts affect them all, and not only the young couple that had "selfishly" opted to marry of their own accord.

Society and family crisis

As stated previously, inter-caste marriages cause inordinate number of problems for the couples and the communities in question. On the one hand, those who accept an incoming bride from a different caste or religion face the consequences of both abuse and harsh treatment from all sides, and on the other hand, the ones who lost a daughter have cause to be abused because they could not marry their daughter in accordance to tradition. In the case of a high caste woman marrying a groom from a lower caste, the groom's community is apprehensive. Causing confusion due to one's unaccepted behavior or actions is not tolerated precisely when the rules are jumbled, prompting members to assert modes of behavior contrary to those they are socialized to observe towards higher caste people. For the lower caste, having to readjust is a problem especially since the daughter-in-law would be incorporated into their own *gotra*. Should they redo the kinship rules for conduct? This issue was brought to my attention many times during the research, in particular when the bride came from a much higher caste. A 14-year-old girl said that she had no idea what she had assumed in marrying against her parent's wishes, as she was totally incapable of understanding what she consented to embark on. She adds that she was young and had no practical sense of her actions. She felt that she wasted her early life. "I firmly believe that when parents arrange marriages for their children, they look around, discuss and then select the matches. My life would have been happier had I married according to the choice of my parents. They would have been responsible towards me, and shared in my happiness and sorrow. As I have had an 'inter-caste love marriage' that I engaged in against their wishes they have no duty or responsibility towards me" (Meera Interview 2004). Her reaction resonates with the level of abuse she endures from her husband whom she willingly chose to marry despite her parents' objections. She lost the right to complain about her condition and her right to return to her father's house when she chose a love marriage. Today, she begins to understand and to recognize the value of arranged marriages.

In the past, marriage was the primary concern for a young unmarried woman. Given the challenges women faced in the past and which are very much part of the present crisis women experience today, they have been forced to rethink their priorities. The increase in inter-caste marriages alerts a traditionally restrictive society to what some of the women's fears and concerns are. Perhaps establishing and finding gainful employment could replace the women's anxieties, or having to learn what the proper code of conduct should be for a woman could be of importance.

Doing research in Bengal, I was invariably made aware of encounters to do with the empowerment of women, especially that which is transferred to the women through religious agency. Pondering over debates of women's strength, oftentimes the reference alludes to women's sacred power which complements male divine power, the *shakti/prakriti* model of male and female unity. Even though one comes to understand the meaning of women's strength, one is equally aware of their tendency to be naturally subservient to their husbands. They are socialized to be obedient, expected to remain close to their tradition and upbringing. They are to serve the family first before all other concerns. According to Piyush, "She is bound to obey the 'order' of her husband whether right or wrong. Because women like me do not have economic freedom, we are dependent on the income of our husbands. Until the time when women become financially self reliant, they are bound to depend on their husbands. (Women with employment) are able to enjoy freedom in society. She is not dependent on her husband and so has the power to protest if he does anything wrong. Men respect and are slightly scared of their 'service holder' wives" (Piyush Interview 2006). Being dependent on her husband, a married woman is forced to cater to him, always giving in to his demands. Women are astute, knowing where and when they can negotiate and when they should give in. In contrast to the men, women are cognizant of society's power over families and their lives, enforcing the rule of the majority on the individual. Lakshmi, a married woman who gave up her personal dreams after marriage says, "We can't do anything minus society. Our 'next generation' will follow our footsteps. If I lead a reckless life my 'next generation' will do the same. It will be bad for me; and during negotiations for my daughters' wedding there will be many problems. I will find it difficult to arrange their marriages. If a family earns a bad reputation once, it becomes very hard for their girls to have good marriages. Nobody wants to arrange matches with girls from a family of ill repute. Our thoughts are limited to this area as well. My daughters' weddings will be negotiated within this town, not outside. That is why we have to obey the social rules" (Raj, Lakshmi's husband, Interview 2005).

For the reason that a married woman is financially dependent on her husband, it is incumbent that she panders to his demands; a married woman knows that she is required to cater to her husband. An outspoken woman who married against her parents' wishes and made no dowry offers to her self-selected husband finds that she relies on him financially. He is the sole earner in the family. Due to her situation, she adds that she is careful not to antagonize her husband, affirming that "I am certainly scared lest there be any discord at home. And to avoid that, I don't ask or pressurize him to do any work. To me, household peace is very important. To keep it I'm willing to 'sacrifice' everything" (Meera Interview 2004). She clearly articulated the underlying fear, which is still prevalent within the families. Meera's comments confirm that self-reliant women having their own income enjoy a lot of freedom in their parental homes, where they exercise their liberty before and after marriage, more so compared to unemployed "housewives." "Until women are self-reliant, earning herself—their misery will never end. It can be seen in reality that those educated women who have good jobs and earn well have good marriages and spend their lives in peace and happiness. They do not have any poverty or need. They can bring up their children well and send them to good schools and colleges for education" (Piyush Interview 2006). Torture or the violence of dependency, as some women consider their fate, hinges on the ability of the woman to provide more after the marriage, more so in the case of those women who were married with the gift of a dowry. Love marriages take place because of one's right to choose their own husband. In this situation the couple does not discuss the question of dowry payments prior to the marriage. Having to care for a wife and having one who is fully dependent on a man raises apprehensions and expectations about compliance and obedience to the head of the household. One's socialization and ideals come into focus, and usually men become forceful about maintaining decorum and a close approximation to societal and family ideals by reintroducing outdated culture and gender-based codes of conducts. On the other hand, we found that young unmarried girls have awakened and begun to take matters in their own hands. Facing their dilemmas, where they are culturally constructed as divinities and yet are exposed to violence and death threats, they seek solutions to abate the brutalities. The choices they make are socially reviled, and yet they refuse to remain silent to the abuse they experience or have heard about through the media or word of mouth. They have managed to confront the issues facing them. Young women have spoken to me in ways that their mothers did not thirty years ago, breaking the habit of silence, a tradition that in their eyes strangled their mothers before them. They know that legally they neither have to accept nor are they expected to withstand violence. What they aim to resolve are ways of educating themselves in order to disengage with the existing cultural disparity between the genders, to disaffiliate from beliefs that render them powerless. Unlike their mothers before them, this generation is astute and aware of their limitations as women. They understand that simply accepting their predicament is not going to assist them in moving forward. They ask as to why they, women, are considered to be less than men, and why they are left with no options such as those which a Western woman uses to fight to establish and assert herself. Nonetheless, not all the girls who marry against their families' approval, against their religious principles, caste and community's trepidations are fighting against tradition.

Quite a few of these "gone astray" marriages end up recreating new traditions or following their husband's norms.

In conclusion: Questioning societal ideals and its consequences

Violence against women seems to pervade the recent scholarship coming out of India. Scholars are addressing these and related questions in a variety of forms: literary published works, popular culture (songs, scroll paintings and most poignantly street plays) or asking what the political parties/scene has done lately to address the women's question. In a volume edited by Bishakha Datta (2010), the essays address the question of justice and whether women's lives have improved in the recent past. Has justice been accorded to the victims of rape and violence? Do women have the right to choose a partner despite parental and community objections? And if so, who protects these women? A few of the authors dwell on the question of the violence women silently tolerate. Similar queries are raised in the volumes edited by Chandra Mohanty (1991 and 2003) and in Navaneetha Mokkil and Shefali Jha's work (2012). How has the state safeguarded the rights of women? Which states provide better facilities regarding protection and offering safety to women marginalized and cast out of their families? Does the West Bengal state offer women protection and address their repeated abuse and violence?

The consequences of inter-caste and inter-religious marriages today are inordinate. Inter-caste marriages cause unnecessary problems for the couples, as well as to the communities in question. Families accepting a bride from a different caste or religion expect the woman to bear the consequences of abuse and harsh treatment from them, whereas the family which has lost a daughter is subject to abuse for not marrying their daughter in accordance to tradition. Parents are incriminated for failing to advice their daughter who went astray. In the case of a woman from a high caste marrying a man from a lower caste, the groom's community is apprehensive about the ensuing chaos which is caused when the kinship rules are jumbled. Lower caste families are confronted with a predicament of having to readjust, especially since the higher caste daughter-in-law would have to be incorporated into their own *gotra*, and the confusion leaves them at an initial loss. This issue was brought to my attention many times during the research, precisely when the incoming bride was from a much higher caste. The joy of receiving a bride in these cases trigger tremendous constraints and oftentimes fear of being misunderstood. On the other hand, the inter-religious unions generate problems on an enormous scale. Crossing over religious boundaries, for a woman to convert to a new religion in an effort to be welcomed as a new family member frequently exposes her father's family to animosities and rivalries with her in-laws. I have heard of stories where families observing different religious faiths but who were friendly to each other in the past have stopped talking or interacting with each other when one of their sons married one of their daughters. The shared sentiments will give way to daily harassments and accusations, taunting the various members especially if the Hindu girl converts to Islam after the marriage. When families who feel betrayed by a son or daughter, have to explain the loss of a child to strangers, they find it an unpleasant experience. However, somehow, these frustrated families felt they could trust me with their stories. I became a confidant to their unexpressed emotions towards an opposing community or to a particular family, for they had no qualms unleashing their strong emotions or aversions to a total stranger. Simply put, the marriage of their daughter, the conversion to a new religion, which they do not understand or want to accept, creates the strong emotions that they begin to express towards their daughters-in-law. These intense feelings of anger and pain surface and, in some cases, bring up Partition narratives that evoke historical India/Pakistan divide, or the rape and abduction of Hindu women by Muslim men. All of these chronicles develop to address and to make sense of why one's Hindu daughter would marry a Muslim man and convert to his religion. Explaining the actions of a daughter who turned her back on her family's religion and tradition will never suffice, nor will it be accepted. Initial pain is replaced by anger and at times retribution. Some families resort to the law, but no family has taken back a daughter after her marriage, whether she married outside of her caste or her religion. Nevertheless, the verbal expression of vehemence against the marriage is unending. Few families will learn to accept such distasteful marriages, and most will remain reluctant. Although for some a total acceptance of the marriage is impossible, a few try to extend a supporting hand and initiate a semblance of a relationship with their daughter and her children (not necessarily embracing her new family). If the affected families turn around and fully accept the untraditional unions of their sons or daughters, it will surely threaten their standing within their community. Accepting a child's error, forgiving their actions, will be considered to be a judgment call. The forgiving parents will jeopardize their own standing; forgiving their children can easily place heavy unresolved social responsibilities on themselves, which will transpire in the future. Instead, most of these families tread carefully lest their own communities too shun them.

The freedom to choose leads many young men and women to take a bold step and choose their life partners. A few did so as to justify their right to actually exercise their choices. Others feared the consequences of being married to families who might not treat them kindly. Some understood the financial difficulties facing their parents and were opposed to paying a dowry for marriage. Those who expressed their antipathy to paying a dowry for marriage were forceful in making the point that women should be treated as equal to men, and that women were not a "marketable commodity." I would not add here that I was in the midst of a growing feminist movement. I came across limited expression of the concept in my interviews, yet attaining empowerment and its multiple signification was expressed more often than being a feminist. The irrelevance of feminism was more the norm, and here I agree with Kamla Bhasin's interpretative work on the topic (Bhasin and Khan 1999; see also Chakravarty 2003; Bullbeck 1998; Code 1991). Expressing a move away from tradition would not warrant us labeling them as a radical group or a generation of new-formed feminist women. Many would end up paying close attention to tradition, or to the correct way to behave after their marriage (even though the union causes anxieties and disruption to families). A few of these couples seek "respect" and acceptance, reminiscent of their mother's past (see Forbes excellent 2005 essay). Young couples living in a society where the norm is to be a "part of" a family, community, religion or caste, find it rather difficult to "just be," as some, explain. I found many of these couples expounding a more conservative way of living and a stricter future for their children, some vehemently opposed to allowing them the choice for a marriage partner. Somehow, the idea of tradition is more in focus, stronger and forceful. As a woman reiterated about marriage, "Women dream from their childhood about a home; they always nurture a wish of being a mother. Because of this strong desire of being called a mother, women have a greater tendency to get married. That is why a woman would get married to any man" (Priya Interview 2006). Indeed, young women and men have been known to trigger a series of unjustified events, which their communities find offensive. We must assume that these actions, without the intention of causing the couples' families pain or malice, are the only alternative available for most women. Returning to a life in which nothing has changed before their unacceptable marriage, or living in the same town and wishing to reside in their familiar area is denied to them. As the first step of their denial (a reminder that they no longer belong to their original communities), the couple begins to reposition themselves in new residential settings. They attempt to emulate what they have left behind, a kind of social convention that could ingratiate them back to the families they lost along the way. The journey back is slow, careful and, at times, succeeds in attempting to undo their initial objectionable actions. Families begin to cultivate them and accept their children who are marked as members of their father's family. Asking if there was change, if the freedom to choose was a prime mover here, if in fact tradition was replaced, the answer would be mixed. My conclusion is that indeed young couples made a choice, took a different type of journey and later returned to a life which, though somewhat new, was yet acceptable to members of the community. The future of the children born of these marriages is resolved so that instead of being marginalized, they are accommodated into their father's community. In a sense, one returns to the source, perhaps not to what was originally mapped out for them, but to an acceptable position, given their parents' marriage situation. Taking up the only charted tradition, one safeguards the future of the children born in these problematic unions. In addition to the fear of violence on oneself, women also fear the unresolved future for their children and this protectiveness underscores their expressed vehemence when the children's future comes up in discussions.

In concluding this discussion on the topic of violence, and to address the national awareness of violence, what comes to one's mind is the question of the ideal type of woman and its significance today. What went wrong and how is it that the idealization and victimization of women coexist at the same time? Women wonder how the same society juxtaposes the two views—violence and sacredness on one another. A second question that kept coming up during my research is the issue of violence within and outside one's place of birth. If marriage is a sacred act and if women are to be given in marriage as gifts to men outside of one's blood line, moving to a new household and abiding by their rules for conduct, why is it that women who are necessary for a father to enact the most important responsibility face the hardships on account of marriage—the same act which the father is so proud to be responsible for? Finally, with regards to the legal system, there are women officers appointed to handle rape and violence against women. Yet not many victimized women take advantage of those particular units within the police stations. Not all cases seem to receive the same attention and priorities from the police. Muslims complain that their cases against Hindus are not taken seriously, but cases coming from a Hindu against a Muslim become a priority to the police. Speaking to cases addressing violence and brutalities, those women who seek legal action against their husbands, express that their cases are viewed as lower in terms of priority for the police. So how serious is the law in combating and averting violence against women?

Notes

1. Bina trained in music, learned to play various instruments, and became a great vocalist under her father's guidance. She went on to receive many national and international awards.

Not the Final Word on Indian Women: Can she speak for herself?

> *Women are an integral part of the nationalist discourse, thus to think of the nation is to recall the symbol upon which the image was constructed.*
>
> *The Indian woman, her femininity, is constructed in tandem with her counterpart, her complementary other, the masculine.* (Fruzzetti 1993)

Marriage defines a Hindu woman, although that is not the case for Muslim women. Thinking about the construction of gender for a Hindu woman, we return to the importance of marriage as the crucial life cycle rite. This rite marks the woman, one who straddles two houses, lineality, and lives. Born as the daughter of a line, she will leave her father's house to embark on her final journey one day. A marriage causes this break; symbolically, a woman severs her ties from her father's line of descent. Additionally, she leaves her place of residence, a home where she was born, nurtured and socialized to understand that her life is yet to begin as a different person, a wife in her husband's home. As a married woman she discards her kinship codes of conduct to adopt new ones, she is the wife of line who is expected to take on new responsibilities and understand the implication of what *sampradhan* means. She is the gift given through marriage witnessed by the gods, ancestors, family and her new affines. She was the gift that established the new alliances between the two families, thus allowing the continuity of her husband's line through the birth of their future children. Immediately following the birth of one's daughter, the inordinate and major concerns for the girl child is to orchestrate making the arrangements for her marriage within one's caste and religion while at the same time being cognizant of the *gotra* rule. Marriages of daughters is more than a problem for a father, it is a cumbersome burden to bear. Unmarried girls have reversed the duties of their elders and caste members.

This book examines notions and meanings of female agency, and how we come to understand marriages enacted outside the bounds of one's own traditional and religious lines. Within India's neo-liberal context, and set against the backdrop of an ever increasing demand for dowry, what impels a woman to choose a way out of an impasse concerning her marriage possibilities to take a path contrary to her family's tradition? How do societies interpret women's "unacceptable actions" regarding their choice of a partner for marriage?

Marriage is the most sacred Hindu life cycle rite. The rites of marriage are complex endeavors involving multiple agents in the final decision for what constitutes an acceptable partner in marriage. What drives or causes an unmarried woman to deny her society or caste members the right to decide her marriage partner? Why are the Hindu principles and structures of marriage inflexible and uncompromising when it comes to alternatives in choosing a partner?

Young girls negotiate multiple interlocking structures, cognizant that by asserting their agency they come into conflict with the sacred aspects of their socialization, the challenge they pose affects the parental power over their children, most importantly in deciding their marriage alliances (Fruzzetti 1982; Karp 1986). A self-selected choice of partner in marriage does not (or might not) attest to societal, caste, and occasionally religious sense of acceptability. Women articulate their newfound agency, although liminal in symbolic terms; the freedom to "act," to "break away" from familiar to uncharted territory (physically and symbolically) is lived experience. Once she enters a new household as a wife she submits to their tradition. Agency and the ensuing difficulties in the context of a modern day woman will nonetheless rest on traditional mode (see Mokkil and Jha 2012; Bagchi 2009). In fact, self selecting a husband or wife beyond one's restricted and endogamous group, similar to the Huli females in New Guinea, ". . . implies conceit, defiance, and 'self-importance'—both in the sense of arrogance and in the sense of making one's individual self the final arbiter of one's choices" (see Leavitt 1998, quoted in Wardlow 2006: 4). Women who choose without consulting or obtaining permission to marry outside the bounds of the accepted familial dictates are denounced publicly as being self-righteous and selfish in their selection of a spouse. These "lost," "arrogant," "selfish" or "self-important" women, as they are referred to by their caste members, are women who draw their momentary agency by deliberately severing from kinship and caste-based notion of what constitutes a person. "Persons are thus only fleetingly and provisionally unitary actors, for they are always oriented toward and moved by the relationships in which they are embedded and of which they are made" (ibid: 7). To break those ties freely, dissolving ties with one's culturally embedded identity, one's grounding in society and caste, in matters concerning the meaning of a woman/man, apprises us of a tragic break; at times such a break disallows a return to one's family. Gita Aravanundan raises very difficult questions demonstrating that despite being a woman defined through her culture, her expectations as a proper woman has proven unsuccessful today given the "seeming irrational" marriage decisions that young girls make; with or without employment, women are making their own decisions (Aravanundan 2010; Kumar 2011). When women discard the elements that forge a person's being, most importantly the makings of a proper woman, those actions elicit the ire of kin and caste members. Drawing on Marilyn Strathern's work in Melanesia, the kinship similarities regarding the construction of the person or the idea of a person in Bengal, positions culture and kinship as central to the symbolism of what constitutes the person (1988: 13). Societal concerns seem to be acute when women transgress the familial codes of acceptability, more so than the actions of men for the simple reason that women ". . . are considered to be the custodians of cultural particularisms by virtue of being less assimilated, both culturally and linguistically, into the wider society" (Kandiyoti 1991a: 382).

Referring to Östör, Fruzzetti and Barnett's (1982/1992) work on the Bengali construction of the person and what symbolizes the individual, unmistakably one can comprehend the serious offences caused when tradition is transgressed or kinship matters are ignored. Worst is the injury and ruins to a family having to face the conversion of a daughter to a different religion. Hindu marriages are intricately connected to caste; in fact central to the rite is caste endogamy. An untraditional marriage where a couple defies caste and religious lines, crossing those boundaries demarcates the woman's marginality to her family (see Chowdhury 2007). Today, young women's refusal to follow the tradition of their parents, of their mothers who previously unquestioningly imbibed a culture of tolerance, is at the center of discussion, seeking a more empowering and less marginal role for themselves as women (Chakravarti and Panjabi 2011).

Moreover, severance from familial or caste relationships, when understood through the context of blood connectivity, further highlights the seriousness of the offence. Offering a daughter to one's affines is a father's right. The sacred act of giving her in marriage is denied to her father's line when she makes her own choices to marry. More egregious is the offence when she marries outside her caste and religion. Unmarried girls have come to ignore the attachment to culture, tradition or religious principles; they undoubtedly do not privilege the cultural construction of the person or the tradition of women they were socialized to assimilate (see Östör, Fruzzetti and Barnett 1982/1992; Östör and Fruzzetti 1984 and Fruzzetti and Östör 1998). We find instead women who have "awakened" their self as individuals, detached from imposed cultural barriers. Women are meant to follow their fathers and forefathers, act as ". . . heirs to other persons who formed and cared for them, and their personality is revealed both in their relations to others and in response to their recognized genesis" (Code 1991: 85). Women willingly transgress kinship and caste boundaries knowing they will be marginalized from their kin and home.

Undeniably, women's roles are crucial to the alliances of families involved, the ongoing tradition of the particular lines, nurturing of children and maintenance of household and continuity of values and beliefs. At the same time we come to understand women's efforts and challenges, their reaction against the prescriptions set for them.

Women have transcended the mark of being the guardians and preservers of tradition, they have moved beyond those essentialized, docile and accommodating roles they so clearly were associated with and have come to represent. When a woman condemns or criticizes her traditional or her family's ways of conducting marriages and hers in particular, she censures instead of emulating a Sita-like ideal womanhood. Raheja and Grodzins state that characterizing women as repressed and silent is not the complete picture of an Indian woman today, ". . . submission and silence may be conscious strategies of self-representation deployed when it is expedient to do so, before particular audiences and in particular contexts" (Raheja and Grodzins 1994: 11). A woman was not given the right to speak nor to decide her future, she was portrayed ". . . as a silent shadow, given in marriage by one patrilineal group to another, veiled and mute before affinal kinsmen, and unquestioningly accepting a single discourse that ratifies her own subordination and a negative view of femaleness and sexuality" (ibid: 4).

Young girls have confronted this view; instead of the silent demure image epitomizing a woman, they dared to speak up and go against the ways of their mothers before them. Enforcing their need to change and their right to choose their marriage partners, these couples who defied the norm, the structure of tradition, do so knowing that they are outside of the controlling boundaries; they in fact acquire a kind of freedom (and often use the concept to define or describe their actions). They are denounced and shunned from their communities, they find themselves thrown into an anti-structure world, an unfamiliar space which they have created through their defiant actions, which places them close "with non-social," to use Turner's dichotomies. The liminal (anti-structure) or the "fantasy-rejection of structural necessities" is the world that they are forced to inhabit until their return back to normal time and space (Turner 1982: 45). I use the concept of liminality to describe the phenomenon a man and a woman create for themselves while they recast their new life through an unwanted and unrecognized marriage by their communities, ". . . the breakdown without compensatory replacement of normative, well defined social ties and bonds" (ibid: 46).

Obstructing the principles of one's culturally imposed ". . . set of regulatory practices that seek to render gender identity uniform"; they purposefully deviate from the ideal feminine model of actions reflecting "the good woman" (Moore 1999: 155). "Yet women's stake in nationalism is far more complex than the foregoing suggests. On the one hand, nationalist movements invite women to participate more fully in collective life by interpolating them as 'national' actors: mothers, educators, workers and even fighters. On the other hand, they reaffirm the boundaries of culturally acceptable feminine conduct and exert pressure on women to articulate their gender interests within the terms of reference set by nationalist discourse" (Kandiyoti 1991b: 443). Thus, to impose their will and enforce a self-defined agency, unmarried girls go beyond the "contained structures" crafted for a woman's domain, refusing to be subordinated in a socially restricted space which implies subordination of females and where ". . . their bodily energies and their agency are meant to be encompassed" (Wardlow 2006: 12). Adult marriageable women refuse to be "controlled" or manipulated as property, a few respond by negotiating their own decision-making while others use alternative methods. The actions of engaging in inter-caste or inter-religious marriages are premeditated. Women do not act impetuously; what prompts them has more to do with matters of the heart. Self-motivated (often secretive) acts of unorthodox marriages cause extreme anguish to one's family and society. An act taken clandestinely will nonetheless challenge kin male members' authority and caste associations, once the marriage is made public. Undoubtedly, women have arrived at a juncture of life where their self-interests override the hierarchical and kin-based power imposed on them. Exerting her own personal agency, a woman acts alone, empowered to go beyond her boundaries knowing full well that she lacks protection; ". . . such acts of refusal are often self-destructive. The withdrawal or excision of bodily capacities from the social body can entail the elimination of these capacities altogether" in that her decision to act on her own "... is another form of this negative agency in which a woman severs from the social group that which should most be encompassed by it—her sexuality" (ibid: 15). Using the concept of "negative agency" (see Kratz 2000; Wardlow 2006) women fight the imposed gender-based rule by negating their socialization. A woman appropriates "agency," though temporary and liminal, to make her own start in life; the discord is with her culture and traditional dictates. Her injurious act to her kin can be permanent; her freedom to act is transitory, liminal, linked to anti-structure (not connected to a specific structured time). After her marriage/union her free will is curtailed; if she persists in exercising her autonomy or "personal found agency" it will create turmoil in her life. Married women succumb to the new social order in their life, be it new caste rules or the religion of one's husband.

Bengali society places value on women, on the gift of the daughter in marriage, in setting an alliance. "What most defines women as women, then, is the subordination of their sexuality to the larger project of social reproduction" (Wardlow 2006: 17). A woman given as a gift in marriage to one's new alliance-based group sets in motion an enduring system of relationship joining a selected family in marriage where, as a bride, a woman then follows their kinship and religious prescriptions (Fruzzetti 1982 and 1998).

What binds descent lines is the gift of the virgin, whereas self-initiated unions or marriages across unaccepted boundaries work against the "culture of acceptable unions." Fathers of unmarried girls navigate the appropriate and "correct' unions for his daughter, by marrying her to a chosen line who will further regulate her sexuality. Fathers give a daughter away in marriage conducted in accordance to caste and religious lines. When a girl makes her own choice of a partner, her act is self-centered, not socially or culturally orchestrated, and it goes against all set norms. Her undertaking denies alliance through marriage within their social, religious or familial boundaries and denies the gifting of the dowry along with the bride. Although one presents a positive side to giving of dowry, or *stridhan* (a woman's wealth), dowry today has shifted meaning and focus. Dowry ". . . is transacted between men of two families, and the control over a woman's dowry lies not with her but with her husband and his family" (Menon 2012: 42) In Menon's recent book, she reiterates what I found to be the case regarding dowry during my earlier research on marriages in Bengal. It seems very little has changed, in fact the growing ". . . violence associated with dowry—its non-voluntary character, oppressiveness and systematic dowry related violence against women in their marital homes" (ibid: 40) has become compounded. Young girls understand the perils of arranged marriages, they deviate from the accepted norm and choose alternatives which are challenged.

The self, one's individual choice irrespective of breaking cultural norms, replaces the social. Women are meant to observe their status prescribed by their cultural understanding of what constitutes a woman in and out of marriage. Women are either daughters or wives of a line; a woman experiences two journeys in life, something that every Hindu woman endures. Taking matters as serious as marriage in one's hand, opting to take a self-selected path of autonomy instead of the socially constructed and accepted mode of action, revokes her inherited socialization process. Her momentary sense of agency or freedom translates into a different value, beliefs, rules or guidance to a new construction of gender. It is different; it will be rearranged to highlight a new tradition, one that she will learn after her marriage. As a married woman, she is unable to renounce patriarchy. A wife inherits that which is of her husband; his world becomes hers irrespective of what her own personal priorities or choices might be.

The citizen/woman and her rights:
Discourse beyond kinship and tradition

Going beyond cultural dictates or the familiar world, to journey beyond the acceptable terrain, women draw on their rights as citizens. Their movements, their undesirable choices, cannot fall within the signification of the domestic boundaries; instead they reflect an opposition to tradition, actions devoid of cultural sanctions. How do we come to understand the woman/citizen? What is the woman's question today? Has the assumption that ". . . the wife is the husband's property, a passive object over which no other man has rights" still the status quo? (Menon 2012: 38). Is this one of the many reasons that young women opt to make their own choices for marriage, when and to whom they want to be married to?

Women reiterate that the objectionable actions are at times the last resort. Maitrayee Chaudhuri contends that we do not find the necessary changes one sought and hoped to right women's positions. "It has been argued that the women's question itself became a site for defining what tradition is . . ." (2003: 360) though women activists did challenge this approach and mold for women. To entertain major transformations to tradition would necessitate revolutionizing how we think about the nation, tradition and women. Continuing her argument Chaudhuri states that ". . . if 'the nation is the home and home is the mother' women cannot but be signifiers of ethnic/national difference. They participate centrally in the ideological reproduction of the collectivity and as transmitters of its culture" (Chaudhuri 2003: 358). On the other hand, Mahua Sarkar's (2008) discursive analysis on the colonial and nationalist period adds that the category "woman" itself and the question of agency are deficient. She refers to Kamala Visweswaran's work (1994), who argues that we need to revaluate what the "domestication of women" means and how to interpret its meaning. Kandiyoti's (1991a) study contributes to the discussion of "private" and the "domestic" adding, "The definition of household and kin-based controls over women as 'private' presupposes the existence of a central state apparatus that subordinates such entities to its own political ends. Likewise, it is an entirely different matter for a woman to be subject to the customary strictures of a community which happens to be Hindu or Muslim and quite another for her under a regime that has adopted one or another faith as a source of public policy, social legislation and national identity" (Kandiyoti 1991a: 378). Continuing this debate, Mahua Sarkar adds that we need to question inherited definitions and constructions for gender and its limitations, we ". . . ought not to be read as a mere by-product of a nationalist 'strategy for contesting colonial hegemony,' as some scholars have contended, but also as an explicit ploy to curb the agency of women and file it down to dimensions that suited the needs of men and their nations" (Sarkar 2008: 7).

Focusing on women through the prism of the private, the household, or as custodians of tradition, this crucial role is less about empowerment and instead marginalizes the woman. This scenario is challenged by younger women, those about to make sense of their future on their own terms. Kandiyoti reminds us that the ". . . demands of the 'nation' may thus appear just as constraining as the tyranny of more primordial loyalties to lineage, tribe or kin, the difference being that such demands are enforced by the state and its legal administrative apparatus rather than by individual patriarchs (Kandiyoti 1991a: 377). Though the nation is symbolized and represented as a woman, their image and ". . . centrality to the nation is . . . reaffirmed consciously in nationalistic rhetoric where the nation itself is represented as a woman to be protected or, less consciously, in an intense preoccupation with women's appropriate sexual conduct" (ibid). Young marriageable girls, knowing what society expects of its women, spurn what is considered to be the appropriate and correct code of conduct for women. To deviate from the model, to modify this symbol and present an alternative has proven problematic to them as well as to their society. "The very language of nationalism singles women out as the symbolic repository of group identity" (ibid: 382). Kandiyoti draws from Anderson's (1983) seminal work on kinship-based definitions of the concept of nationalism, motherland and the idea of home/nation parallels. Thus, following along those lines we come to understand that the idea of "nationness" is to be ". . . equated with gender, parentage, skin-colour—all those things that are not chosen and which, by virtue of the inevitability, elicit selfless attachment and sacrifice" (Kandiyoti 1991a: 382).

I started this chapter by reiterating that marriage defined a Hindu woman, and that in Hindu society a woman's identity is grounded by caste and religious principles. Although young women inform me to the contrary, I am not totally swayed by the conviction of their words and ideals. Indeed, they are selecting their own partners, "defining tradition" as they state, or empowering themselves in the choices they make. Their attempts to transgress and violate tradition or the will of their elders has been ground for much of the debates and disgruntlement within the communities affected by these unaccepted marriages. Rebelling against tradition was done by marrying secretively contrary to one's family, caste or religious injunctions, but none of these couples have settled into a life out of the bounds of convention and dictum deemed acceptable to the communities in question. The initial upheaval is often resolved, not always amicably, but the birth of children can cement over the tensions and affront the couple experience when their marriage is made known. In time, the wounds heal and families come to terms with the decision either a daughter or son has chosen. Crossing religious lines tends to require a much longer period for reconciliation between parents and children, less so in the case of inter-caste unions.

Glossary of Indian and Bengali words

alta:	a red lac dye used by women to color the sides of their feet
acar:	a rite; traditional observance; a custom
adhikar:	a right; responsiblity
amader-swadhinata:	our freedom, our right
ashouch:	pollution; impure; impurity
atmahatya:	suicide
bari:	a house; household
Bauri:	one of the lower castes
brata:	a form of symbolic ritual act; a vow; a contract between a person and a deity
burkha:	a long black cape like dress, worn by Muslim women to cover their body
Durga:	Mother goddess
fatwa:	religious opinion, or decree
ghar:	a house; household; dwelling
ghat:	open edge of water where daily bathing, washing, and also ritual activities are done
gotra:	titles of seers, or rsi, said to have originated in the distant past; constituting a maximal descent label
haram:	religiously forbidden

hijab:	Muslim dress
Jamiat-il-Islam:	a community of Muslims
kalma:	Arabic phrase recited as a declaration of belief to become a Muslim
kazi:	Muslim religious leader
kayastha:	one of the upper Hindu castes
kurta:	a knee-length, loose upper garment
lakh:	100,000
loha:	iron; refers to the iron bangle worn by Bengali married women
lohar:	made of iron
mahr:	Muslim bride price given by the groom to the bride side
maulavis:	Muslim priest
meyder:	of women; belonging to the women's world
namaz:	Muslim prayers
niyom:	customs and laws
para:	neighborhood
paisa:	coins of the Indian currency
prakriti:	male divine power; created world; nature
prasad:	offerings from the gods
puja:	an expression of honor and respect through rituals; a form of worshipping deities
purdah:	physical, gender segregation observed between men and women; veil worn by women to cover their head
Sakti:	female divine power
salwar:	loose, baggy pants
sampradan:	the sacred gift of the virgin in marriage by her father
sankha:	conch shell; here refers to a conch shell bangle worn by Bengali married women
Santhal:	a tribe of eastern India
sindhur:	vermilion powder worn on the forehead and the *sinthee*, the parting of the hair, by married women as an auspicious item
talaq:	Muslim divorce

Bibliography

Anderson, Benedict. 1983. *Imagined Communities: Reflections on the Origin and Spread of Nationalism*, London: Verso.

Aravanundan, Gita. 2010. *Indian Women at Work*. New Delhi: Penguin Books.

Bagchi, Anita. 2009. *Changing Faces of Indian Women*. Kolkata: Levant Books.

Banerjee, Gooroodas. 1915. *The Hindu Law of Marriage and Stridhana*. Calcutta: SK Lahiri.

Basu, Srimati. 1999. *She Comes to Take Her Rights: Indian Women, Property and Propriety*. Albany, NY: State University of New York Press.

Bhasin, Kamala and Nighat Said Khan. 2004. "Some Questions on Feminism and its Relevance in South Asia." In *Feminism and India*. Ed. Maitrayee Chaudhari. New Delhi: Kali for Women.

Bhattacharya, Sreeparna. 2007. "Interrogating Violence: Uncovering Silences—Investigating Marital Violence in India." Doctoral Dissertation, Brown University, Providence, RI.

Bishakha. Ed. 2010. *Nine Degrees of Justice; New Perspectives on Violence Against Women in India*. New Delhi: Zubaan.

Bloom, Ida, Karen Hagemann and Catherine Hall. Eds. 2000. *Gendered Nations: Nationalisms and Gender Order in the Long Nineteenth Century*. Oxford/New York: Berg Publishing.

Bullbeck, Chilla. 1998. *Re-orienting Western Feminisms: Women's Diversity in a Postcolonial World*. Cambridge: Cambridge University Press.

Butalia, Urvashi. 2006. "Gender and Nation: Some Reflections from India." In *From Gender to Nation*. Ed. R. Ivekovic and J. Mostove. New Delhi: Zubaan. 99–112.

Chakravarti, Paromita and Kavita Panjabi. Eds. 2011. *Women, Gender and Culture in India*. Kolkata: Stree.

Chakravarty, Uma. 2003.*Gendering Caste through a Feminist Lens*. Calcutta: Stree.

Chatterjee, Partha. 1993. *The Nation and its Fragments: Colonial and Postcolonial Histories*. Princeton, N.J.: Princeton University Press.

Chaudhari, Maitrayee. 2011. *The Indian Women's Movement: Reform and Revival*. New Delhi: Palm Leaf Publications.

———. 2004. "Introduction." In *Feminism and India*. Ed. Maitrayee Chaudhari. New Delhi: Kali for Women.

———. 2003. "Gender in the Making of the Indian Nation-State." In *Sociology of Gender: The Challenge of Feminist Sociological Knowledge*. Ed. Sharmila Rege. New Delhi: Sage Publications. 341–366.

Chowdhury, P. 2007. *Contentious Marriages, Eloping Couples: Gender, Caste and Patriarchy in Northern India*. New Delhi: Oxford University Press.

Code, Lorraine. 1991. *What Can She Know? Feminist Theory and the Construction of Knowledge*. Ithaca: Cornell University Press.

Das, Veena. 2000. *Violence and Subjectivity*. Berkeley: University of California Press.

Datta, Bishakha. Ed. 2010. *Nine Degrees of Justice; New Perspectives on Violence Against Women in India*. New Delhi: Zubaan.

———, Meenakshi Shedde and Sharmila Sathye. Eds. 2001. *And Who will make the Chappatis*. Kolkata: Stree.

Dumont, Louis. 1980. *Homo Hierarchicus: The Caste System and its Implications*. English edn. Chicago: University of Chicago Press.

Forbes, Geraldine. 2005. "The Politics of Respectability: Indian Women and the Indian National Congress." In *Women in Colonial India: Essays on Politics, Medicine and Historiography*. New Delhi: Chronicle Books.

Fruzzetti, Lina. 1998. *Women, Orphans, and Poverty: Social Movements and Ideologies of Work in India*. Quebec: World Heritage Press.

———. 1993. *The Gift of a Virgin: Analysis of Women, Marriage, Ritual, and Kinship in Bengali Society*. With a new introduction. 3rd rept. New Delhi: Oxford University Press India.

———. 1982. *The Gift of a Virgin: Women, Marriage, and Ritual in a Bengali Society*. New Brunswick, N.J.: Rutgers University Press.

———. 2006. "Women, Culture and the Feminized Nation: The Woman's Question." In *On Foreign Ground: Essays on the Importance of Barely Perceptible Structural Codes*. Ed. Minna Ruckenstein and Marie-Louise Karttunen. Finnish Literature Society: Studia Fennica Antropologic, New Series.

———— and Ákos Östör. 2007. *Singing Pictures: Art and Performance of Naya's Women*. Lisbon: MuseuNacional de Etnologia.

———— and Ákos Östör. 2003. *Calcutta Conversations*. New Delhi: Chronicle Books.

———— and Ákos Östör. 1990. *Culture and Change Along the Blue Nile: Courts, Markets, and Strategies for Development*. Boulder: Westview Press.

———— and Ákos Östör. 1998. "Hierarchy Revisited." In *Changing Patterns of Family and Kinship in South Asia*. Ed. Asko Parpola and Sirpa Tenhunen. Helsinki: StudiaOrientalia, Finnish Oriental Society.

———— and Rosa Maria Perez. 2002. "The Gender of the Nation: Allegoric Femininity and Women's Status in Bengal and Goa." In "Minds of the Empire: Towards a Debate," *Ethnographica*, VI (1): 41–58.

———— and Sirpa Tenhunen. Eds. 2005. *Culture, Power, and Agency: Gender in Indian Ethnography*. Kolkata: Stree.

Huq, Shireen P. 2005. *Bodies as Sites of Struggle: Naripokkho and the Movement for Women's Rights in Bangladesh*. London: Zed Books.

Ivekovic, Rada and Julie Mostove. Eds. 2006. *From Gender to Nation*. New Delhi: Zubaan.

Jayawardena, Kumari and Malathi de Alwis. Eds. 1996. *Embodied Violence: Communalising Women's Sexuality in South Asia*. London: Zed Books.

Jeffrey, Patricia and Amrita Basu. 1998. *Appropriating Gender: Women's Activism and Politicized Religion in South Asia*. New York: Routledge.

———— and Roger Jeffery. 1996. *Don't Marry Me to a Plowman! Women's Everyday Lives in Rural North India*. Boulder, Colorado: Westview.

Jeffrey, Roger and Alaka Malwade Basu. 1996. *Girl's Schooling: Women's Autonomy and Fertility Change in South Asia*. New Delhi: Sage Publications.

Kabeer, Naila. Ed. 2005. *Inclusive Citizenship: Meanings and Expressions*. New Delhi: Zubaan.

Kandiyoti, Deniz. 1991a. *Women, Islam, and the State*. Philadelphia: Temple University Press.

————. 1991b. "Identity and its Discontents: Women and the Nation." *Millenium: Journal of International Studies*, 20 (3): 429–43.

Kapadia, Karin. Ed. 2002. *The Violence of Development: The Politics of Identity, Gender and Social Equality in India*. London: Zed Books.

Karp, Ivan. 1986. "Agency and Social Theory: A Review of Anthony Giddens." *American Ethnologist* 13 (1): 131–37.

Katrak, Ketu. 2006. *Politics of the Female Body: Post-Colonial Women Writers of the Third World*. New Brunswick, NJ: Rutgers University Press.

Kratz, Corrine. 2000. "Forging Unions and Negotiating Ambivalence: Personhood and Complex Agency in Okiek Marraige Arrangement."

In *African Philosophy as Cultural Inquiry.* Ed. Ivan Karp and D.A. Masolo. Bloomington: Indiana University Press. 136–71.

Kumar, Raj. 2011. *Women Empowerment: A Key to Development.* Delhi: Neha Publishers & Distributors.

Leavitt, Stephen. 1998. "The *Bikhet* Mystique: Masculine Identity and Patterns of Rebellion among Bumbita Adolescent Males." In *Dangerous Words: Language and Politics in the Pacific.* Ed. G. Herdt and S. Leavitt. New York: New York University Press. 85–107.

McClintok, Anne, Aamir Mufti and Ella Shohat. 1997. *Dangerous Liaisons: Gender, Nation and Post-Colonial Perspectives.* Minneapolis: University of Minnesota Press.

Menon, Nivedita. 2012. *Seeing like a Feminist.* New Delhi: Zubaan.

Menon, Ritu. 2006. "Do women have a country?" In *From Gender to Nation.* Ed. Rada Ivekovic and Julie Mostov. New Delhi: Zubaan. 43–62.

Millas, Sara and Reina Lewis. 2003. *Feminist Post Colonial Theory: A Reader.* New York: Routledge.

Miller, Diane. 2004. *Rape and Race in the Nineteenth-century South.* Chapel Hill: University of North Carolina.

———. 1999. "Wife Beating in India: Variations on a Theme." In *To Have and to Hit: Cultural Perspectives on Wife Beating.* Ed. Dorothy Counts, Judith Brown and Jacquelyn Campbell. Urbana: University of Illinois Press. 216–33.

Mohanty, Chandra Talpade. 2003. *Feminism Without Borders: Decolonizing Theory, Practicing Solidarity.* Durham: Duke University Press.

———, Ann Russo and Lourdes Torres. 1991. *Third World Women and the Politics of Feminism.* Bloomington: Indiana University Press.

Mokkil, Navaneetha and Shefali Jha. 2012. *Thinking Women: An Introductory Reader.* Calcutta: Bhatkal & Sen.

Mongia, Padmini. 1996. *Contemporary Post Colonial Theory: A Reader.* London: Arnold.

Moore, Henrietta. 1999. "Whatever Happened to Women and Men? Gender and Other Crisis in Anthropology." In *Anthropological Theory Today.* Ed. Henrietta Moore. Cambridge: Polity Press. 151–71.

Narayan, Uma. 1997. *Dislocating Cultures: Identities, Traditions, and Third World Feminism.* New York: Routledge.

Östör, Ákos and Lina Fruzzetti. 1984. *Ritual and Kinship in Bengal.* New Delhi: South Asia Publishers.

———, Lina Fruzzetti and Steve Barnett. Eds. 1992. *Concepts of Person: Kinship, Marriage, and Caste in India.* With a new introduction. Repr. New Delhi: Oxford University Press India.

————, Lina Fruzzetti and Steve Barnett. Eds. 1982. *Concepts of Person: Kinship, Marriage, and Caste in India.* Cambridge, Mass.: Harvard University Press.

Petteman, Jan Jindy. 2005. "Globalization and the Gendered Politics of Citizenship." In *Women, Citizenship and Difference.* Ed. N. Yuval-Davis and P. Werbner. London: Zed Books.

Pilot, Sara and Lora Prabhu. Eds. 2012. *The Fear that Stalks: Gender-based Violence in Public Spaces.* Delhi: Zubaan.

Raheja, Gloria Goodwin and Ann Grodzins Gold. 1994. *Listen to the Heron's Words: Reimagining Gender and Kinship in North India.* Berkeley: University of California Press.

Rau Badami, Anita. 1996. *Tamarind Mem.* Toronto: Penguin Books.

Ray, Sangeeta. 2000. *Engendering India: Women and Nation in Colonial and Post Colonial Narratives.* Durham: Duke University Press.

Rege, Sharmila. Ed. 2003. *Sociology of Gender: The Challenge of Feminist Sociological Knowledge.* New Delhi: Sage Publications.

Sarkar, Mahua. 2008. *Visible Histories, Disappearing Women: Producing Muslim Womanhood in Late Colonial Bengal.* Durham: Duke University Press.

Sarkar, Tanika. 2001. *Hindu Wife, Hindu Nation: Community, Religion, and Cultural Nationalism.* Bloomington: Indiana University Press.

Sen, Satadru and James H. Mills. 2004. *Confronting the Body: The Politics of Physicality in Colonial and Post Colonial India.* London: Anthem Press.

Singh, A.K. 2011. *Crimes Against Dalit Women.* New Delhi: DPS Publishing House.

Sriram, Rajlakshmi and Arun Bakshi. 1988. "Family Violence Against Married Women." *Social Change* 18 (3): 45–48.

Strathern, Marilyn. 1988. *The Gender of the Gift: Problems with Women and Problems with Society in Melanesia.* Berkeley: University of California Press.

Sunder Rajan, Rajeswari. 2004. "Rethinking Law and Violence: The Domestic Violence (Prevention) Bill in India." *Gender and History,* 16 (3): 769–93.

Thapar-Bjorkert, Suruchi. 2006. *Women in the Indian National Movement: Unseen Faces and Unheard Voices, 1930–1942.* New Delhi: Sage Publications.

Thapar, Suruchi. 1993. "Women as Activists, Women as Symbols: A Study of the Indian Nationalist Movement." In "Nationalisms and National Identities," *Feminist Review,* 44 (Summer): 81–96.

Turner, Victor. 1982. *From Ritual to Theatre: The Human Seriousness of Play.* New York City: Performing Arts Journal Publications.

Ulbrich, Patricia and Joan Huber. 1981. "Observing Paternal Violence: Distribution and Effects." *Journal of Marriage and Family*, 43 (3): 623–31.

Visweswaran, Kamala. 1994. *Fictions of Feminist Ethnography*. Minneapolis: University of Minnesota Press.

Wardlow, Holly. 2006. *Wayward Women: Sexuality and Agency in a New Guinea Society*. Berkeley: University of California Press.

Yuval-Davis, Nira and Pnina Werbner. Eds. 2005. *Women, Citizenship and Difference*. New Delhi: Zubaan.

Index